The Madeleine Investigation:
Incompetence or Corruption?

WHY ARE MADELEINE'S ABDUCTORS STILL AT LARGE? WE ASK QUESTIONS THE PORTUGUESE POLICE MUST ANSWER.

The Justice for ALL the McCann family forum

authorHOUSE®

AuthorHouse™ UK Ltd.
500 Avebury Boulevard
Central Milton Keynes, MK9 2BE
www.authorhouse.co.uk
Phone: 08001974150

First published by AuthorHouse 4/23/2009

ISBN: 978-1-4389-5780-7 (sc)

This book is printed on acid-free paper.

WRITTEN BY MEMBERS OF THE 'JUSTICE FOR ALL THE McCANN FAMILY' FORUM.

CONTAINS PREVIOUSLY UNSEEN PICTURES AND DOCUMENTS!

Justice For **All** The McCann Family.

ABOUT THE AUTHORS

This book has been compiled and co-written by a group of members of the 'Justice for all the McCann family' internet chat forum http://justice4mccannfam.5forum. biz/forum.htm. This is an unofficial and wholly independent forum, in no way related or connected to the McCann family, their friends or any official support group. Our forum was set up to show support for the McCann family, and offer aid, in whatever way possible, to help in the search for their daughter, Madeleine, still missing at the time of going to print.

The forum also engages in discussion of the latest developments in the case, is highly critical of the failed investigation to find her, and happily dismembers the fanciful, far fetched, hurtful and in many cases libellous theories and comments from other forums that appear to revel in her disappearance and enjoy adding to her parent's suffering.

We consider these sites to be the internet equivalent of the street corner or shopping parade, where the local ignorant, poorly educated and undisciplined yobs hang out, intent on causing as much havoc and pain on any one they see as weaker than themselves. We don't like bullies, and we will continue to stand up to them, for as long as it takes to find Madeleine, and reunite her with her loving family.

1. A NOTE TO THE PORTUGUESE PEOPLE.

There are some forums on the internet, those dedicated to persecuting the McCann's without trial, without evidence, who would have you believe that anyone who criticizes the investigation into Madeleine's disappearance must somehow be xenophobic, or racist. These individuals will hear no word of censure against the PJ or their disgraced former chief, Goncalo Amaral. They will try and tell you that the McCann family and all their supporters hold some sort of grudge against the whole of Portugal, and therefore, it's people.

We would like to take this opportunity to assure you that nothing could be further from the truth. We have no argument with the good, honest and welcoming people of Portugal. Our argument is purely and simply with those individuals in authority, and in particular Mr Amaral, who were most directly involved with the early part of the investigation, who leaked lies and smears, contrary to your own strict secrecy laws. Who failed to follow up many sightings, some of them highly credible. Who lied to the parents of a missing child, assuring them they were not considered suspects, when from day one they were working on the opposite judgment, to the total exclusion of all other options. Who lied about DNA evidence, and distorted the value of sniffer dog indications. Who made the parents suffer almost a year of torment as Arguido's, without so much as a scrap of evidence.

We would be equally fulsome in our condemnation of our own police forces if they had behaved in a similar fashion.

2. PREFACE: THE SALLY CLARK EFFECT.

From the 'Justice for all the McCann family' forum.

Writing something on another thread on a different subject made me think about Sally Clark, a woman who had a good education, from a good family, some would say a 'privileged upbringing'. She made her way in life and enjoyed a certain status that her and her professional husband had gained through education, application and hard work.

How unlike Kate and Gerry McCann was the Clarks status? When you start reading what happened to Sally Clark, for me it made me realise what could have so easily happened to Kate and Gerry McCann. And how there are parallels between what happened to Sally and what happened to Kate. Fortunately Kate was not charged, but this was not for want of trying by some in the echelons of Portuguese power and law. The case of vanished, believed abducted Madeleine McCann, had the propensity to be one of the biggest miscarriages of justice the world had seen, if it had ever got as far as a Portuguese court of law, and I base this on what happened to Leonor Cipriano and her brother Jaeo Cipriano, and their convictions for the murder of Joana Cipriano, on what appears to be the flimsiest of circumstantial evidence.

From Wikipedia.

Sally Clark (15 August 1964 – 15 March 2007) was a British lawyer. She was the victim of a miscarriage of justice; her convictions in 1999 for the murder of two of her sons were quashed in 2003.

Clark's first son died suddenly within a few weeks of his birth in 1996. After her second son died in a similar manner, she was arrested in 1998 and tried for the murder of both sons. Her prosecution was controversial due to statistical evidence presented by paediatrician Professor Sir Roy Meadow, who testified that the chance of two children from an affluent family suffering Sudden Infant Death Syndrome (also known as cot death in Europe or crib death in North America) was 1 in 73 million, which was arrived by squaring 1 in 8500 for likelihood of a cot death in similar circumstance. In an unusual intervention, the Royal Statistical Society wrote to the Lord Chancellor saying there was "no statistical basis" for Meadow's conviction.

Clark was convicted in November 1999. The convictions were upheld at appeal in October 2000, but after she had served more than three years of her sentence, they were quashed in a second appeal in January 2003, and she was released from jail. Journalist Geoffrey Wansell called Clark's experience "one of the great miscarriages of justice in modern British legal history." She was found dead in her home on 16 March 2007.

An only child, she was born as Sally Lockyer in Devizes. Her father was a senior police officer with Wiltshire Constabulary and her mother was a hairdresser. She was educated at South Wilts Grammar School for Girls in Salisbury. She studied geography at Southampton University, and worked as a management trainee with Lloyds Bank and then at Citibank.

She married Steve Clark, a solicitor, in 1990, and she left her job in the City of London to train as a solicitor. She studied at City University, London, and trained at Macfarlanes, a city law firm. She moved with her husband to join the law firm Addleshaw Booth & Co in Manchester in 1994. They bought a house in Wilmslow in Cheshire.

Her first son, Christopher, was born on 22 September 1996. Apparently a healthy baby, he was found dead in his cot at 11 weeks old on 13 December. Suffering from post-natal depression, she consoled herself with alcohol. After counselling at the Priory Clinic, she was in recovery by the time her second son, Harry, was born on 29 November 1997, three weeks premature. However, he was also found dead at eight weeks on 26 January 1998. On both occasions, she was at home alone with her baby, and there was evidence of trauma, which could have been related to attempts to resuscitate them.

She and her husband were both arrested on 23 February 1998 on suspicion of murdering their children. **On the advice of her lawyers, she twice refused to answer questions,** and was charged with two counts of murder. **She always denied the charge, and was supported**

throughout by her husband. She gave birth to a third son in 1999.

She was tried at Chester Crown Court, before Mr Justice Harrison and a jury. The prosecution was controversial due to the involvement of the paediatrician Professor Sir Roy Meadow, who testified at Clark's trial that the chance of two children from an affluent family suffering cot death was 1 in 73 million. **He likened the probability to the chances of backing an 80-1 outsider in the Grand National four years running, and winning each time.**

She was convicted by a 10-2 majority verdict on 9 November 1999, and given the mandatory sentence of life imprisonment. **She was widely reviled in the press as the murderer of her children.** Despite recognition of the flaws in Meadow's statistical evidence, the convictions were upheld at appeal in October 2000. She was imprisoned at HMP Styal, near her home in Wilmslow, and then HMP Bullwood Hall in Hockley in Essex. **The nature of her conviction as a child-killer, and her background as a solicitor and daughter of a police officer, made her a target for other prisoners.** Her husband left his partnership at a Manchester law firm to work as a legal assistant nearer the prison, selling the family house to meet the legal bills from the trial and first appeal.

Later, it came to light that microbiological tests showed that Harry had colonisation of staphylococcus aureus bacteria, suggesting that her second son may have died from natural causes, but the evidence had not been disclosed to the defence. **This evidence had allegedly been known to the prosecution's pathologist, Alan Williams, since February 1998, but had not been shared with Clark's defence team. This evidence was unearthed by the divorce lawyer Marilyn Stowe, who provided her** services free of charge because she felt "that something was not right about the case". Dr Williams was found guilty of serious professional misconduct by the General Medical Council in June 2005, for a number of reasons but particularly for his **incompetent** postmortems on both babies. Dr Williams appealed this decision to the High Court but in November 2007, **the High Court upheld the General Medical Council's ruling of serious professional misconduct.**

It also became clearer that the statistical evidence presented at her trial was seriously flawed. Her case was referred back to the Court of Appeal by the Criminal Cases Review Commission, and she was released from jail in January 2003, after serving over three years of her sentence. Her convictions were formally quashed in a second appeal in January 2003.

Her case led to a wide-ranging review of hundreds of similar cases. Two other women were cleared of similar charges.
According to her family, she was unable to recover from the effects of her conviction and imprisonment. After her release, her husband said that she would "never be well again." She was unable to read John Batt's book based on her case, Stolen Innocence: A Mother's Fight for Justice. In 2005, Meadow was struck off the medical register by the General Medical Council for serious professional misconduct, but he was reinstated in 2006 after he appealed.

Clark was found dead in her home in Hatfield Peverel in Essex on 16 March 2007. It was originally thought that she had died of natural causes, but an inquest ruled that she had died of acute alcohol intoxication, though the coroner stressed that there was no evidence that she had intended to commit suicide.

Statistical evidence

The case has been much criticised because of the way statistical evidence had been misrepresented in the original trial, particularly by expert witness Sir Roy Meadow, former Professor of Paediatrics at the University of Leeds. **He stated in evidence as an expert witness that "one sudden infant death in a family is a tragedy, two is suspicious and three is murder unless proven otherwise" and that the chances of two Sudden Infant Deaths in the same affluent, non-smoking family were 1 in 73 million.**

Looking at this case and the case of Madeleine McCann and how her parents have been persecuted by the baying crowds who abide by some kind of 'mob rule', it seems to me that the same laws of 'INjustice' are at work.

The McCanns have their very own self proclaimed expert, Tony Bennett, who thinks nothing of meting out his own wholly inaccurate opinions, based on supposition and the ramblings of an ex cop, and any other unsubstantiated rumour he can pick up. The ex-cop himself retired under a cloud, and who, as stated earlier, is now facing his own trial for alleged offences against yet another mother, who has been convicted of murdering her child on the flimsiest of evidence, (if it could ever be termed 'evidence').

What are the credentials of one Tony Bennett, that he can seek to give his 'opinion' in the forum of a booklet, that he hopes to distribute? Looking at his history, he seems to be a bit of an attention seeking 'Jack of all trades and master of none', sort of person. Someone who appears to thrive on publicity, and who appears to want to be allowed to spread his own 'opinions' around, without accepting that others have the right to their own 'opinions'.

From what I can ascertain, Mr Bennett, does not seem to me to be qualified in giving those opinions, especially when those opinions have been based on exactly the same evidence that led the prosecutor in Portugal to declare that there is 'NO' case for the McCanns to answer!

As an EX solicitor, albeit an EX solicitor who was actually found to have brought his profession into disrepute by the 'Law Society', perhaps Bennett, nontheless, should be able to grasp the concept of this paragraph taken from the Sally Clark files.

She and her husband were both arrested on 23 February 1998 on suspicion of murdering their children. On the advice of her lawyers, she twice refused to answer questions, and was charged with two counts of murder. She always denied the charge, and was supported throughout by her husband.

Sally Clark acted on the advice of her lawyers, as did Kate McCann. 'Advice' given by people who had a full grasp of the 'facts' and were in a position to give such advice. Tony Bennett should take note of this as he is NOT in receipt of the full facts of what happened. Which makes him a very dangerous person in my opinion and certainly not a person who should think himself in a position to go writing books to try and subliminally 'suggest' to the readers, that he in some way knows what happened to Madeleine McCann, while no one else in authority does. He appears to be using his knowledge of the law and the use of certain words to 'suggest' that Madeleine 'probably' died in the apartment that night. In fact this phrase, in some form, is on his signature every time he makes a post on a law forum.

So what is Bennett, trying to 'suggest'?

The only person or persons that do know what happened to Madeleine, are those who abducted her and those that played a part in that abduction on the peripherals, and until those person/persons are hunted down and apprehended, it is unlikely we will know what truly happened to that innocent child.

This is why some of us want a a full and open 'Public Inquiry' carried out in Portugal by those independent of that country.

It is the way things are done, it is the way the civilised society tries to get to the truth, when there are many inconsistencies and unanswered questions by the law enforcers themselves, as there undoubtedly and indesputably are, in the investigation into the disappearance of Madeleine McCann.

We do not want EX-solicitors and EX-cops running around giving us their tainted, one sided versions of what happened surrounding Madeleine's disappearance in the form of books. This is not justice, this is not truth seeking, this is the spreading of inaccuracies, half truths, innuendos, smears and is in some cases outright lies.

How low have we sunk as a civilised society when we allow ex-cops to write and publish books and to benefit from their failures? Failures of which there are many and are 'officially' documented.

An ex-cop who found himself in charge of a case he should never have been allowed anywhere near and failed again to bring the true criminals to justice, and then is allowed to go and write books pertaining to know what happened to Madeleine McCann.

One question: If Goncalo Amaral, knew what happened to Madeleine McCann, why did he not do anything about it when he had the chance?

Why did he not take all the evidence he now points to in his book and simply do something about it, when he was in charge of this case? After all he had 4 months to do it and he failed and he failed comprehensively simply because he could find no evidence.

Does it occur to the likes of Goncalo Amaral and Tony Bennett, that there is an absence of evidence to say that Madeleine's parents harmed their daughter because there is NO evidence and there is NO evidence, because they did NOT do anything to harm their beloved child?

Or is this undisputed fact that there is no evidence to 'suggest' wrongdoing, (one of the few in this case), just ignored and refused to be acknowledged because, if Amaral and Bennett ever did acknowledge this, then like the case of Sally Clark's 'so-called' expert, their whole reason to write their books comes crashing down around their shoulders?

In that case all they would be left with is spite, incompetence, jealousy, avarice and total failure.

3. INTRODUCTION.

I can't imagine that anyone reading this book would need any reminder of what happened on the night of May 3rd, 2007, in the Portuguese resort town of Praia de Luz. Madeleine McCann, just a few days short of her fourth birthday, vanished from her bed, presumed by most sensible people to have been abducted. Her abduction was remarkable for many reasons, not least of which was the way it dominated the media for almost a year, with scarcely a day going by without the leading British newspapers having a front page headline about some aspect of the case.

But beneath the still unsolved mystery of her disappearance, and the obvious and unyielding attempts of her parents to find her, there began to grow an undercurrent to the whole story. There began to appear a growing unease, suspicion even, about the way the police investigation into Madeleine's abduction was being handled. The British media began to use words like incompetent, blundered, shambles and mishandled. Indeed, the head of Scotland Yard is on record as saying the whole investigation was 'botched and bungled' from day one.

Is this criticism really fair? After all, the Portuguese police were dealing with a very difficult case, with no apparent clues or leads to work on. Surely they were just doing the best that they could, under very difficult circumstances?

We say that not only is the level of scorn poured on the police justified, it doesn't go far enough. We believe the standards of this investigation fall woefully short of any level considered acceptable in a civilised society, but worse, we suspect there may possibly be corruption involved; perhaps even, at some level, a degree of complicity or involvement with child smuggling rings within Portugal and further abroad. We say this, we believe, with some justification.

Let us start with the former police chief in charge of the case, Goncalo Amaral. In Great Britain, if a Chief Constable had allegations of witness intimidation and torture brought against him, he would be suspended, with immediate effect, until the allegations were either proved or discredited. If those allegations involved the beating of the mother of a missing girl, that would make it even more imperative that the accusations be speedily resolved, in order that the search for that missing girl could be put back on track, with the minimum of delay. Mr Amaral has had just those sort of accusations levelled at him. He has been accused of, and at the time of writing is standing trial for, covering up the torture of Leonor Cipriano, whose daughter Joana, went missing on September 12, 2004, only seven miles from where Madeleine was abducted. And yet, while he was being investigated for this alleged involvement, instead of being suspended, he was put in charge of ANOTHER case of a missing girl, this time a foreign national. This, to us, is incomprehensible, as it goes completely contrary to the standards of police accountability we are familiar with in this country.

In this book we will cite other cases of missing children, and the Portuguese authorities reaction to, and handling of, these cases, raising serious questions about the competency of the Police forces, and will hopefully show you, the reader, there is enough compelling evidence to demand a public enquiry into the way Madeleine's abduction was investigated.

4. Portugal, a brief history.

On the 25th April 1974, the longest fascist Dictatorship in Europe, lasting for almost 5 decades, was ended by a military coup, now referred to as the Carnation Revolution.

Up until this time, for over 40 years, Portugal was ruled by the Authoritarian regime of Antonio Salazar. Salazar became Portugal's Prime Minister in 1932 and ruled until ill health 1968.

In 1933, Salazar introduced a new constitution to Portugal, which gave him wide powers, establishing an anti-parliamentarian and authoritarian regime that would last four decades.

When Salazar came to power, the regime evolved into a classic fascist dictatorship heavily influenced by the corporatist ideas of Benito Mussolini in Italy. This was evidenced in the formation of the Estado Novo.

Salazar developed the "Estado Novo" (literally, New State). The basis of his regime was a platform of stability;

his reforms were advantageous to the upper classes while detrimental to the poorer sections of society. Education was not seen as a priority and therefore not heavily invested in. Salazar relied on the secret police (often known by the name it carried from 1945-1969, PIDE) to repress, torture and, in extreme cases, murder dissidents.

Another change happened in 1945, the Policia De Investigacao Criminal which was founded in 1867 changed its name to the now famous **Policia Judiciaria**. Many people still believe the legacy of the Estado Novo and the methods they employed are still alive and kicking within the PJ.

In view of the above, it is not surprising to learn that Amnesty International was formed after the experience of its founder who encountered examples of torture in Portugal.

Even as late as 2003 Amnesty International were bringing to the attention of the Human Rights Committee concerns about reports of Human Rights violations in Portugal.

http://asiapacific.amnesty.org/library/index/en-geur380012003

Jumping forward to 2007 and the police investigation into the disappearance of Madeleine McCann.

As well as growing fears that Madeleine was abducted by a paedophile ring, the McCann's can have little hope of justice when leading Portuguese figures are allegedly involved in covering-up their own child sex scandal.

Both cases - the two highest profile criminal investigations in the country since the end of the Portuguese military dictatorship in 1974 - have been riven by allegations of compromised police officers, high-level interference and vicious, virulent attacks on key witnesses.

Pedro Namora, a former Casa Pia orphan who witnessed 11 rapes on fellow orphans, during which they were tied to their beds, sympathises with the McCanns. He believes elements in the force have conspired to suppress both scandals, fearing damage to the country's reputation.

"Portugal is a paedophiles' paradise," said Mr Namora, now a lawyer campaigning on behalf of the Casa Pia victims. "If all the names come out, this will be an earthquake in Portugal. There is a massive, sophisticated network at play here - stretching from the government to the judiciary and the police.

"The network is enormous and extremely powerful. There are magistrates, ambassadors, police, politicians - all have procured children from Casa Pia. It is extremely difficult to break this down. These people cover for each other, because if one is arrested, they all are arrested. They don't want anyone to know."

Now 44, Mr Namora watched as friends sank into alcoholism, drug addiction and death after their traumatic childhood experiences at Casa Pia. "I was the only one who made it," he said. "What could I do? I couldn't keep silent."

He has received death threats and warnings about what will happen to his own children, after taking up the case when an orphan called "Joel" approached him, saying prominent paedophiles were using Casa Pia as a "supermarket for children".

Mr Namora has been threatened after fighting on behalf of the abused children he grew up with.

After being telephoned by a stranger offering to pay off his mortgage, he was told the exact movements of his own three children, and warned that they and their father would come to a grisly end unless he shut up.

An open, warm man, Mr Namora makes an unlikely conspiracy theorist-But he believes the case, which he brought to light in 2003, will underscore **Portugal's growing attraction for paedophiles,** which has seen six children disappear in recent years.

One reason for this attraction is that the law was quietly relaxed last year, ahead of the forthcoming trial, meaning that repeat offences against the same child would merit only a single charge - and a lesser sentence.

In echoes of the McCanns' ordeal, the initial investigation was badly handled when allegations of abuse were first made at Casa Pia in 1982. Carlos Silvino, the man known as Bibi, was linked to rapes and assaults, but police "lost" pictures showing prominent Lisbon politicians with him and the children.

He was only charged after dozens of children came forward in 2003. They also accused Jorge Ritto, a former Portuguese ambassador, of child abuse. Ritto, it transpired, had also once been sent home in disgrace from a posting in Germany after an incident involving a young boy in a park.

The conspiracy did not end there. Teresa Costa Macedo, a former secretary of state for the family, has revealed that she knew about the attacks in the early Eighties - and that she had alerted General Antonio Ramalho Eanes, the then Portuguese president, about the allegations.

Mrs Costa Macedo, who remained silent for two decades after being warned she would be killed if she spoke, now says that the caretaker "was just one element in a huge paedophile network that involved important people in our country. It wasn't just him [the caretaker]. He was a procurer of children for well-known people who range from diplomats and politicians to people linked to the media".

While still a government minister, Costa Macedo handed police "photographs, an account of the methods used to spirit children out of the orphanage and testimonies of a number of children". Many of the photographs were found at ex-ambassador Jorge Ritto's house. Police reportedly found four children locked up who had been missing from Casa Pia.

Under armed guard at a safe house last week, Bibi could count himself a lucky man. He originally faced allegations that he had sexually assaulted more than 600 children. That has since been reduced to 30. Silvino has hinted at the high-level of the conspiracy, saying: "They can't touch me - there are too many people involved."

Following Ritto's arrest, the police questioned Carloz Cruz, known as Portugal's "Mr Television", and Joao Diniz, a high- society doctor and driver of the red Ferrari. The network allegedly went further. Paulo Pedroso, a government minister, was arrested and quizzed about 15 cases of child sexual abuse.

Amid allegations that **paedophile networks have become endemic in Portugal** - the European police force Interpol has named the country **as one of the worst offenders in Europe** - there are fears that the Casa Pia scandal will come to eclipse Belgium's notorious Marc Dutroux case, in which the arrest of a notorious paedophile and child murderer revealed a sordid picture of judicial and political corruption.

Of course, the Casa Pia case may have no direct link to the disappearance of Madeleine, **but the culture in which such a serious child abuse network was allowed to operate is the same culture that pervades the whole of Portugal.** Was it this attitude that led to the bungled initial investigation in the McCann case?

5. CHILD ABDUCTION AND MURDER, SOME PORTUGUESE CASE HISTORIES.

I am going to start this chapter with a deeply disturbing statement. If you were a Portuguese resident, or happened to be staying there on holiday, and you had to suffer the appalling disaster of having a child go missing, the BEST you could hope for is that your local police do nothing to help you. That's right, you read that correctly, the BEST you could hope for. Hope that they do not lift a finger, do not step outside their police station, don't even summon up the energy to raise their backsides of their police station canteen chairs. Does that statement shock you? It should.

Because the worst thing is beyond your darkest nightmare. The worst thing is that they could take you into their cosy little station, charge YOU with your child's murder, beat you so badly that your face looks like a raw hamburger, torture you until you confess to a crime you did not commit, then lock you away. You will receive a travesty of a trial with no evidence produced to back up the police charges, your child will remain missing, perhaps forever, their abductors will remain free, and the world will quickly forget, if it ever even hears about you in the first place.

You may think that an exaggeration, over the top. After all, Portugal is not a third world country, is it? It is a modern democracy, a member of the European Community. You may think such things could never happen in such a country. But you would be wrong. Chillingly wrong.

In order to place the abduction of Madeleine McCann in the right context we regretfully must open your eyes to the shameful history of child abuse and abduction in Portugal, and the official attitude to it. The following may prove to be deeply upsetting to some, and for that we apologise. But these stories MUST be told, a wider public MUST be made aware, because there is something very wrong with the Portuguese justice system.

Our first story involves the Casa Pia state run orphanage. A place of supposed sanctuary for the most vulnerable children of any society, those who have lost their parents. All children should have the right to protection and a good level of care, and an orphanage is supposed to provide such for those who have, for whatever reason, lost the love and support of their immediate family. In short, in such homes they should be safe. Casa Pia, however, was run as a one stop shop, or lending library, to some of the most well connected of Portugal's paedophiles, with claims of abuse being levelled at TV celebrities, judges, government ministers and diplomats. These people would arrive on a Friday, book a child out for the weekend, then return them on the Sunday. Deaf/mute children were preferred, as they would have the hardest job to draw attention to their suffering. As you read the following article, you will see obvious signs of cover-ups, incompetence and behind the scenes deals to keep the rich and powerful protected from justice. This case is, at the time of writing, still ongoing, with as yet no convictions.

http://en.wikipedia.org/wiki/Casa_Pia_child_sexual_abuse_scandal

Although some reports of abuse dates to before the Carnation Revolution of 1974, in 1981, Portuguese Judiciary Police (Polícia Judiciária) accused the caretaker of a Casa Pia state-run children's home of raping dozens of children over a period of 30 years, and supplying children to several men of both Portuguese and other nationalities, including some prominent personalities of Portugal. At the time, Portuguese Judiciary Police had possession of photographs taken by one of four men accused of sexually abusing young children. **These pictures inexplicably disappeared from the police files** and the case against the caretaker was dropped.

The scandal of alleged sexual abuse at the state-run Casa Pia orphanages resurfaced when several former orphanage children came forward with accusations of abuse. The accusations linked some politicians, diplomats, and media celebrities — all of whom were alleged to have conspired in a pedophilia ring that had operated for decades. The scandal broke in September 2002 when the mother of one alleged victim, known as Joel, complained of abuse by staff at a Casa Pia house.

Former Casa Pia children came forward to publicly accuse several personalities of sexual abuse. The weekly magazine Visão reported that a Portuguese diplomat, Jorge Ritto, was removed from his post as consul in Stuttgart (1969-1971) after German authorities complained to Lisbon about his involvement with an under-age boy in a public park.

Accused were diplomat Jorge Ritto, Carlos Cruz (a famous Portuguese television presenter), Carlos Silvino (a.k.a. Bibi, an employee of Casa Pia and a former pupil in the institution) Ferreira Diniz (a physician from Lisbon), Hugo Marçal (a lawyer who was a defendant of Carlos Silvino in the early stages of the process) and among other individuals, a marine archaeologist.

Secretary of State for Labor and Training from 1999 to 2001, Paulo Pedroso, who was responsible for the Casa Pia homes, which care for some 4,600 children at 10 centers around Portugal, was suspected of 15 cases of sexual violence against minors, which allegedly took place between 1999 and 2000. **His case was also subsequently dropped**. In September 2008, a Portuguese court ordered the state to pay 100,000 euros ($140,000) to the ex-minister Paulo Pedroso, on the grounds that he was wrongly detained on paedophilia charges.

The Socialist Party leader at the time, Eduardo Ferro Rodrigues, who was a close personal friend of Paulo Pedroso, offered to undergo police questioning after "he had learned of plans to implicate him in the [Casa Pia] scandal". The weekly paper Expresso published a report on May 25, 2003 from four children who said they saw Ferro Rodrigues at locations where sexual abuse was taking place. The paper said there was no evidence he was personally involved and the Attorney General José Souto de Moura insisted he was not a suspect. Ferro Rodrigues took legal action against those who said they saw him at locations where sexual abuse was taking place. Rodrigues has said, "I want it to be clear: our fight will be serene but determined and it is and will only be directed at those who are responsible for this defamation, whatever their objective is."

The Prime Minister at the time, José Manuel Durão Barroso, whose Social Democratic Party ousted the Socialists in March 2002, promised to bring life and honor back into the Casa Pia child's homes and allow new director Catalina Pestana to reform the institution. As a result, several senior staff of Casa Pia were fired after the 2002 revelations. However, Pestana, told parliament and the media, as late as 2007, that **there may still be pedophiles in the Casa Pia system**. She also criticised the legal changes made after the start of the trial, which she claims **were made in order to help those who were present to court.**

The Casa Pia abuse scandal has had a positive effect of raising public awareness of sexual abuse of children. The number of incidents reported to Portuguese police has soared after the scandal has been revealed.

The Casa Pia child sex abuse trial started in 2004. The final allegations are scheduled for 20th October 2008 in Lisbon.

The country's justice system, often accused of being excruciatingly slow, is believed by some accounts to be vulnerable for external pressures of well-connected personalities and the possibility of corrupting external interference has been considered a real danger, according to critics.

Critics allege that the investigation has been painfully slow. They fear that even if Carlos Silvino (the Casa Pia driver), whose initial trial has been twice postponed, is found guilty, **better-connected abusers may go free**.

RENE HASEE.

The next story is of a German family, on holiday in Portugal. Like the McCann's, their happy days in the sun were to end in tragedy, as they returned home minus one member of their family.

The following is a summary from the 'Portugal Resident,' an English language newspaper for British ex-pats living in Portugal.

This story appeared in the Portugal Resident as the first anniversary of Madeleine's abduction approached. It states how a couple in Germany will be remembering their six-year old son who went missing in the Algarve 12 years ago.

René Hasèe, who was six, disappeared from the Amoreira beach near Aljezur on June 19, 1996. His mother, Anita, a 37-year old postal worker who was on holiday with her partner Peter and René, told a German newspaper at the time: "We had just eaten something and gone down to the beach." It was around 6pm and she said René was around 30 metres in front of her when **"Suddenly our son disappeared as if he had been swallowed by the earth."** After frantically searching the beach for her son, Anita then notified the local police, who, she claimed at the time, **were not very interested and did not bother to search for René, telling her he had probably drowned.**

As with any other missing children cases, the file on René was sent to the Polícia Judiciária, said a GNR spokesman. **But when the desperate parents went to ask on what progress had been made, they found the Lisbon headquarters of the criminal police had no record of René.** In fact they still don't.

"The missing people's database in digital format goes back to 1996," said the spokesman. "The name is not registered on the computer database and we have not found it in the paper entries." However, the spokesman said this does not mean the case is closed. "Sometimes, a case has to wait years until new information is found in connection to it and it is possible this is one of those cases," said the spokesman.

But, just as with Kate and Gerry, this grieving German couple have not given up hope of finding their son.

A young child goes missing, the police can't be bothered to look for him, and when the parents go back to check on the progress, the file is mysteriously 'Lost.' I leave you to draw your own conclusions.

RUI PEDRO.

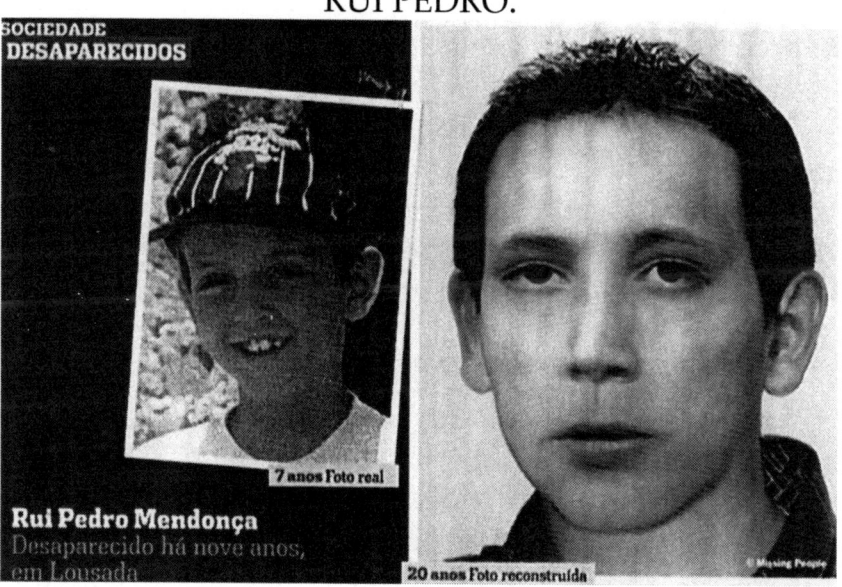

SOCIEDADE
DESAPARECIDOS

7 anos Foto real

Rui Pedro Mendonça
Desaparecido há nove anos,
em Lousada

20 anos Foto reconstruída

Another case of police indifference is Rui Pedro. His mother last saw him on a video, recovered from a Paedophile ring by a European police investigation. Rui was being sexually abused. So far, Rui himself has not been found.

When 11 year old Rui Pedro went missing in Portugal in 1998 all signs pointed to Rui being the victim of an abduction; But when his mother went to the police she was astounded by their attitude.

I went to the Police Headquarters asking for help, because everything was telling us that Rui Pedro was kidnapped and I was told that the Police couldn't do anything. They told me that I would have to ask the judicial district judge to get in touch with the local authorities so we could find out what type of crime this was and only the judge could consider this a kidnapping and only in this case they could interfere. I explained what had happened and implored them to come and act as soon as possible, because on the following day it could be too late

All organisations dealing with child abductions agree that the first 48 hours are crucial. That small window of opportunity can make the difference as to whether a child is found alive or not. This is why the *Amber Alert* in the USA has been adopted successfully in countries like France; it works.

The parent of a missing child in Portugal, however, enters a Twilight Zone where they need to convince the authorities that their child has been abducted. They need to spend those vital hours of that crucial window convincing a local judge that the crime is one of abduction and therefore worthy of police time. Why? Who in God's name does that serve? It doesn't help the parents or the missing child….it *does* help the abductor.

The police should always assume the worst case scenario when a child goes missing and investigate it as a possible abduction, till the facts show otherwise. The onus should be on the police not the parents and bureaucracy should never enter the picture.

Inspite of the judge giving permission for Rui Pedro's parent's phone to be tapped after they received calls asking for a ransom the police refused to accept he had been kidnapped and refused to follow up on the calls;

And every time we asked them if they had followed any clue, they would ask us how could they have done it, if they even hadn't heard these people, nothing could be done in order to know who was calling, as we answered that there are ways to do it, they told us that it was only in the movies.

The response of the police in this case should make every right minded person angry; angry for Rui Pedro, and angry for his parents. Nationality, race and creed become meaningless when a child goes missing, this is not an attack on Portugal. This is about a group of children who were let down badly by a system that makes no rational sense, on any planet.

The police refused to believe that Rui Pedro had been kidnapped until the gates of Hades opened for a second or two to show depravity on an uminagined scale;

Horrific images of Rui Pedro being sexually abused were reportedly uncovered during an international police operation that cracked a global paedophile network. More than 200 paedophiles in 13 countries had exchanged more than 750,000 images of children through a private internet club called Wonderland.

Analysis showed that 1,236 children had been subjected to abuse that officers described as "unimaginable". Some were ba-

bies, raped by their abusers. Others were sexually abused live, to order, on line. Officers described weeping as they catalogued the pictures and being haunted for years afterwards.

The Portuguese boy's mother, Filomena Teixera, flew to Switzerland to view the pictures and was apparently able to identify her son. But he has never been found. The trail has gone cold and investigators fear that may have been murdered to cover up the abuse. Now the disappearance of Madeleine has brought those agonising memories flooding back.

Rui Pedro deserved better than this, as did his parents. His case highlights a pattern in Portugal of dealing with missing children, a pattern that became painfully apparent with the abduction of Madeleine Mccann.

So far, we have seen the kind of callous indifference by some of Portugal's police force that would be unimaginable if it wasn't documented. A cold, blasé attitude to what is probably every parent's worst nightmare. But what if your son or daughter disapeared, and the police DID get involved? What could you expect then? Our next story is of little Rachel Charles, daughter of a British ex-pat couple, living in Portugal.

RACHEL CHARLES

We discovered the tragic case of poor little Rachel and her family on the Anorak website, (www.anorak.co.uk) Rachel disappeared from the resort of Albufeira, thirty miles east of Praia da Luz. It was once a thriving development, favoured by British expats, and included a collection of clifftop villas known as Val Novio.

Now largely abandoned, it was there, on November 19, 1990, that Rachel Charles, aged nine, went missing.

Neil McKay, a Bafta-winning TV scriptwriter who has specialised in factual dramas about crime, was on holiday nearby with his father at the time. "We were sitting in a bar having a beer one evening," he recalled.

"This English guy came in, saying a little girl had disappeared two days earlier but the police were refusing to mount a proper search. He said her family wanted every British tourist or expat to meet on the beach at seven next morning to try to find her.

"so we went. There must have been more than 200 of us. Tragically, it didn't take long to find her body, hidden among some pines."

Len Port, now an Algarve publisher who covered the case for The Portugal News, said: *"The police search was highly inefficient, as, frankly, was everything else about the case. The way the police handled it was desperately amateurish - and ultimately, a travesty of justice."*

Just as they would later do with the McCanns, the PJ, rather than put their effort into proper detective work, and attempt to track down the real murderer, decided it would be easier just to frame someone closer to the family. They arrested and charged a local man. But according to Port, who attended his trial, it had *"no real evidence. It was an unjust trial"*.

The defendant was Michael Cook, a British expat businessman who had taken part in the search, and in 1992 he was convicted and sentenced to 19 years. Having protested his innocence, he was released in 2002. Last week, he told of his ordeal for the first time.

"This has ruined my life," he said. "I still carry the scars from the six times I was stabbed in prison; as for the times I had the s*** kicked out of me, I long ago lost count."

Following Cook's conviction, his MP, Bob Spink, became involved in his campaign. In a Commons debate in 1992, he said: "The only hard evidence linking Cook to the murder was bogus" - a claim by an elderly gardener that he had seen Cook bundling Rachel into his car.

However, Spink said, the police had hidden the fact that tyre tracks left by Rachel's abductor "were of an entirely different type" from those that would have been made by Cook's vehicle.

The PJ, Spink told the Commons, claimed Cook confessed - something he has always denied - and that they had tortured him: "Cook appeared in court, with black eyes and a missing tooth, and he was deeply bruised.

"It is claimed that Cook was hung from an upstairs window by his feet, that his feet were beaten until he could not stand, that he was tied to a chair and beaten, that he was deprived of sleep and that a revolver was forced into his mouth and the trigger pulled in a mock execution."

The PJ also claimed Cook had a record as a paedophile, Spink went on. This, too, was "entirely bogus'.

The trial judge had asked a PJ witness how he knew this: "The officer replied that someone, unnamed, had told him. The judge accepted that so-called 'evidence' as clear and unequivocal."

It emerged at the trial that while there was no forensic link between Rachel or her clothes and Cook's car, blood had been found under her fingernails - presumably that of her attacker. But when Cook's lawyers tried to obtain it to test it for DNA, they were told the samples had been "lost".

Cook told The Mail on Sunday: "I was with the PJ four days and they gave me no food nor let me go to the lavatory - I literally s*** myself and p****d myself. I was in that state when they first brought me to court.

"What I learnt about Portugal is that once convicted, you never get the chance to get it reversed, because they destroyed the evidence."

Spink, who is still MP for Castle Point, Essex, said that as the Madeleine case had unfolded, he had become increasingly concerned by the "disturbing parallels' between the way the PJ had dealt with Maddie and the murder of Rachel Charles.

"In both cases, there was incompetence at the outset. And then, having become convinced they had the right suspects, the police seem to have ignored other avenues of investigation - especially the possibility that both were abducted by a stranger."

After the death of Rachel Charles, it was not for a further 14 years that another girl went missing on the Algarve.

On September 12, 2004, Joana Cipriano, aged ten, failed to return to her home in Figueira, near Praia da Luz, from a shopping trip. **The parallels with the Mc-Cann case are again disturbingly close**.

JOANA CIPRIANO.

Now we come to what is probably the most disturbing and worrying case of all, the tragic story of the Cipriano family. We will go into much greater depth in this case, as it involves none other than the sacked and disgraced former head of the Madeleine enquiry, Goncalo Amaral. We will be using more than one source in this case, as the true depth of this story cannot be fully conveyed in just one piece.

The following is a summary of an article by Alex Watts, of Sky News, that appeared on the Sky news on-line website on Monday, May 12th, 2008. No online link now available.

On the day of Madeleine's fifth birthday, Joana Cipriano's relatives urged detectives to investigate links between the two disappearances - saying there are too many disturbing similarities for the evidence to be ignored.

Joana, eight, was sent to buy some groceries from a village store near her home in Figueira, at around 8pm on September 12, 2004. She bought a tin of tuna and some milk from the Ofelia store, and was last seen by a neighbour walking back near the village church, some 200 yards from her home. Joana never returned and, like the McCanns, her mother Leonor mounted a campaign to find her. Like them, she and her brother Joao became suspects.

The case, which ended with the pair being sentenced to 21 years, made Portuguese legal history - it was the first murder trial where a body was never found. The Police officers involved are currently on trial later for allegedly beating and torturing Leonor to make her confess. Joana's relatives told press reporters the pair are innocent and believe whoever took the girl is also behind Madeleine's disappearance, seven miles away in Praia da Luz. The family, who do not want to be named, said: "Whoever took Joana took Madeleine too, the distance is too small. And the police ignored everything we told them, they just wanted to solve the case quickly. They didn't look at any of the things we told them about." They said the most crucial bit of evidence was a white and brown camper van, parked near Joana's home in the days before she was abducted.

The vehicle, with German number plates, disappeared around the time she vanished. They added: "There was a man living in there, but he hardly left the van. A week later the van was found abandoned in farmland in Praia da Luz. We told the police to investigate it, but they didn't listen to us." She said the man had short, curly brown hair and was about 40 years old. A suspect in the Madeleine case, spotted acting suspiciously near the apartment where she vanished on May 3 last year, was described as between 35 and 40, with long, straggly hair.

Criminologist and child protection expert Mark Williams-Thomas believes there are far too many similarities between the two cases for it not to be a strong line of police inquiry. He says that because of the huge doubts over the Cipriano convictions, whoever abducted Joana is more than likely to be behind Madeleine's disappearance. **Like Madeleine's case, the police investigation got off to a bad start, with officers failing to seal off the house where she was last seen.** Leonor alleges police beat her to make her confess. A photograph of her heavily-bruised face was published in Portuguese newspapers.

Goncalo Amaral, a senior detective who was sacked from the Madeleine case, is one of the five officers charged in connection with extracting the confession. The indictment reportedly alleges that they kicked her, hit her with a cardboard tube, put a plastic bag over her head, and made her kneel on glass ashtrays.

Amaral faces charges of negligence and perjury, another officer is accused of fabricating a document, and the three others are charged with torture.

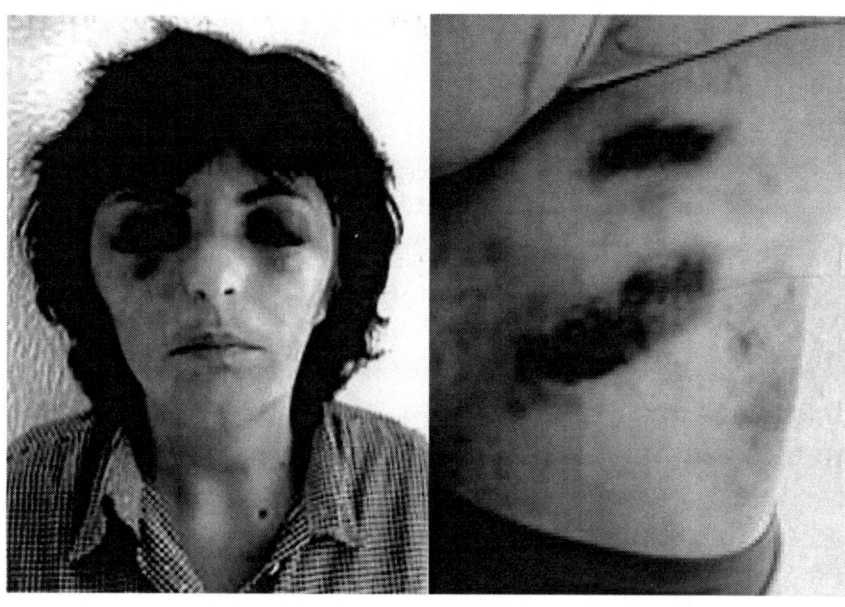

http://minnea.blogspot.com/2008/01/third-link-between-joana-and-madeleine.html

THE top cop in the Madeleine McCann case has been accused of covering up evidence that police tortured the mother of another missing girl into confessing to murder. Leonor Cipriano later recanted her confession, but is serving 16 years' jail for the murder of her daughter, who vanished in Portugal's Algarve region three years ago. The body of Joana Cipriano, 8, has never been found.

Chief Inspector Goncalo Amaral, who heads the Policia Judiciaria in Portimao — the nearest town to Praia da Luz, from where Madeleine vanished — could appear before a secret criminal hearing as early as next month. He is accused of concealing evidence over allegations that three of his colleagues tortured Cipriano, over 48 hours' continuous interrogation, to secure a confession. All four — and a fifth accused of fabricating evidence — deny the allegations. They say Cipriano was injured when she tried to kill herself by throwing herself down police station stairs.

Portugal's police have faced increasing criticism of their handling of the McCann case. Cipriano was unable to pick out any assailants from among the accused officers. Sources say the prosecutor is now investigating the allegation that police paid outside thugs to beat her up. One of the police officers accused of involvement in torture in the Cipriano case is recently retired chief inspector Paulo Pereira Cristovao. He has been writing a daily column on the Madeleine case for a Portuguese newspaper that has been reporting sensational stories leaked **by "sources close to the police inquiry,"** some of which have later proved untrue. He makes it clear he considers the McCanns are probably responsible for Madeleine's death or disappearance.

Like Chief Insp. Amaral, he denies all wrongdoing in the Cipriano case."

Portugal
Report on torture suffered by Leonor Cipriano

Source:
Relatório sobre Tortura de Leonor Cipriano, 8.4.2008,
ACED - Associação Contra a Exclusão pelo Desenvolvi-
mento, SOS Prisoes - report (pdf)

http://www.statewatch.org/news/2008/may/02portugal-
report

SOS Prisões and ACED produced a report that they
sent to high-ranking Portuguese authorities with compe-
tencies in this field concerning the allegations of torture
suffered in September 2004 by Leonor Cipriano at the
hands of the judicial police in their offices in Faro. She is
currently serving a 16-year and eight-month prison sentence in Odemira women's prison, after she was found
guilty of killing her eight-year-old daughter Joana, who
she reported as having disappeared. Cipriano maintains
her innocence and told the author of the report, lawyer
Marcos Aragão Correia, who visited her in prison on 8
April 2008, that there was no evidence to prove the allegations, before describing how she was mistreated for
two days in order to induce her to sign a confession of
this horrendous crime, which she eventually did. Correia
also met the director of Odemira prison, Ana Maria Calado, who confirmed suspicions about Cipriano's treatment, noting that she was "shocked about the conditions
in which Cipriano entered the prison". ACED argues
that it does not have the means to confirm what the situation in terms of the practice of torture by the police in
Portugal may be, but calls on the state to comply with its
international obligations.

Leonor Cipriano's account

After accepting to meet Correia, Cipriano denied having played any part in the death of her daughter Joana, who disappeared on the evening of 12 September 2004 after she went out to buy some groceries for her mother in a nearby shop in Figueira, near Portimão, as she often did. Upon seeing that her daughter was taking longer than expected, she went to the shop and was told that Joana had been there, but had already left with a few groceries, after which the Guarda Nacional Republicana was called. On 25 September, Leonor Cipriano was placed in preventive detention in Odemira prison, and was taken by judicial police officers to their offices in Faro on the next day. She was upset by the allegations made against her (that she had killed Joana, cut her up and fed her remains to pigs), which she rejected. Meanwhile, and in the absence of any evidence, the five officers involved became aggressive, shouted and unsuccessfully tried to convince her to confess, after which the torture began. Two glass ashtrays were placed on the floor, and Leonor was forced to kneel on them, without being allowed to get up until she confessed. She showed Correia the scars on her knees, still visible four years later. She was then sat on a chair with a green plastic shopping bag over her head, and officers started striking her on the head with a cardboard tube, causing her haemorrhages resulting in blood descending to her eyes, and her hands were struck when she tried to take the bag off her head. She was told that she would not get out of there until she confessed, and was made to stand, sometimes with the bag on her head and sometimes without it, and punched and kicked on the side of her ribs, repeatedly.

The torture lasted for two days, after which she signed a confession, and she was then returned to prison, where her serious conditions led to her being taken to Odemira health centre. She was told by judicial police officers to tell the doctor that she had thrown herself down a flight of stairs in the Faro judicial police headquarters in a suicide attempt, threatening that if she spoke of any aggression, she would be interrogated again and would not survive. Cipriano said she did as they demanded in their presence, but told the prison officers and director of the prison what had happened once they left. The director ordered photographs to be taken of her, and for a legal-medical report to be drawn up as a result of her poor conditions. Leonor Cipriano's brother João was also reportedly tortured and found guilty of the murder, although the prison to which he was taken did not run the same checks to determine whether he had been subjected to an aggression. After they were both found guilty, he wrote to his sister to apologise for the lies he had been forced to tell about her. When Leonor was invited to identify her aggressors by an investigating magistrate in Évora in 2006, she was only able to identify one official who was present and did nothing to prevent the abuses, possibly because she had had a bag over her head for long periods, or due to the time that had passed, or because not all her torturers were among the six officers placed before her.

The prison director

Correia then spoke to Odemira prison director Ana Maria Calado, who confirmed Leonor Cipriano's account, noting how shocked she was about her conditions, with black marks, haematoma and bruising in her face, mainly around her eyes, her head and ribs, mainly on her sides.

She assured that the physical marks clearly indicated a violent aggression and not a fall down some stairs, something the legal-medical report also confirmed. She noted that Cipriano's conditions worsened a week after she was tortured, as the blood that had gathered at the height of her brows was so much that it ended up falling over her eyes, leaving her practically blind for almost a month, and the director regrets not having ordered photographs of this period to be taken. She also said that relations between Cipriano and the prison guards and other prisoners were good, and that she did not believe that she had attempted suicide.

Calado expressed her surprise for a number of facts: a) that the judicial police did not take Cipriano to a health centre in Faro to certify that she had fallen down some stairs; b) that the day of her interrogation was chosen during Calado's week of holidays, when she would never have allowed her to be picked up at 6 a.m. without a formal request by the judicial police; and c) that judicial police officers who arrived from Lisbon to investigate the allegations of torture proposed sharing the blame between the judicial police and prison, something she refused. Correia praised the director, describing her as "courageous" and as prizing "values" more highly than "corporate interests".

Conclusion

The report concludes that the testimony of Leonor Cipriano and of the prison director, as well as other available evidence, are convincing in terms of proving that a crime of torture was committed by officers of the Portuguese judicial police. It condemns the use of "medieval methods" to "extract confessions at all cost, even if they are false", as "inadmissible" and as harmful for Portugal's image as an EU member that defends human rights and has a modern legal order and, as such, argues that these practices must be punished in "exemplary" fashion, or the Portuguese citizenry will lose faith in the judicial system.

The report ends with a message from Leonor Cipriano, who was treated as a monster as a result of the horrible nature of the crime she was accused and found guilty of committing:

"I hope that my daughter Joana appears, not only to be with her again, but also to show the world that it was the gentlemen officers of the judicial police who tortured me and who are the real monsters".

As we on the forum took more interest in the Cipriano case, we began to ask questions.

If Leonor tried to commit suicide by throwing herself down a flight of steps, she was presumably in a suicidal state. What steps were taken to monitor or safeguard her welfare in the light of this disturbing incident?

If the blood in the fridge was indeed Joana's, then the fridge itself will have been covered with Joana's DNA. Was *it* ever forensically examined?

At the trial, photographs of the tools used by Joao and Leonor to carve up Joana's body were produced. But what about the tools themselves (We gather, belonging to Joao's father?). Very obviously, they, too, will have been covered with Joana's DNA. Were they recovered and forensically examined?

A 50,000 euro payment was said to have been made to someone within the orbit of the family very soon after Joana disappeared. One unsubstantiated claim is that this was payment for Joana from a paedophile ring. Has this matter been fully and properly investigated?

News made it into the Portuguese press about the blood in the fridge before the veil of secrecy was lifted on the case. How did that breach of secrecy occur?

We began to dig further, and found the following, flimsy evidence was all that was needed in Leonor and Joao Cipriano's trial to convict them of murder. Remember, to this date Joana's body has never been found, or indeed any proof that she is even dead.

It was said that Joana came back and caught the brother and sister having sex and so they decided to kill her so she would not tell their secret. How could this have been accepted as evidence by the court? If Joana was missing, how could the PJ have possibly known what she had or had not seen?

The uncle was seen walking down the road carrying a plastic bag, **and although no one had found such a bag,** and the bag was not searched, a judge **accepted it as evidence** as the PJ said the bag contained Joana's body parts.

It was said that blood had been found in the family freezer and a judge accepted that this was the blood of Joana, but this was NEVER proved as this blood was NEVER DNA tested.

When Leonor's defence lawyer asked for a sample of the blood supposedly found in the family freezer, they were refused, as all samples taken had subsiquently, prior to the trial, been destroyed.

The defence team were refused permission to bring forward as a witness a doctor, who would attest to the fact that the injuries that Leonor sustained were incompatible with a fall down the stairs, as the PJ claimed. (We ourselves spotted a cigarrette burn on Leonor's neck in the photo's. Did she also attempt suicide by burning herself to death?)

If the British police and Crown Prosecution Service had attempted to bring a case to court based on such flimsy, circumstantial and deeply flawed evidence there would be a public outcry. Yet this woman and her brother, by an accident of birth, were born in Portugal. And in Portugal they do things very differently

6. ABDUCTED OR KILLED? THE EXPERT'S OPINIONS.

If Goncalo Amaral is to be believed, then Madeleine died in the apartment. He is on record as saying so, and, despite the complete and total lack of any evidence to back that hunch up, he has even gone so far as to write a book about it, 'The truth of the lie.' The $64,000 dollar question is, 'WHO'S lie?' But, we wonder, who else believes this? Who else is prepared to suspend their grip on reality, and go out on a limb and stand shoulder to shoulder with this ex-cop, and his professional speculation?

There is always, of course, a small but highly vocal minority of less educated people within any society, the sort who are easily led, who don't ask too many questions, and will swallow any old piece of media garbage and believe it as the gospel truth without hesitation. These were the sort of people that the mysterious and so far anonymous 'Source close to the investigation' was aiming for with their campaign of psychological warfare, designed to wear down and break the McCann's with their lies and smears. The sort of people who fell for this constant stream of propaganda are the sort who only ever read the headlines of the daily paper, and never the full article, probably because they contained too many long words. Headlines like 'We can prove they did it!' 'DNA evidence confirms Madeleine is dead!' 'Tapas witness set to change story!' And other sensationalistic headlines. These Mars Bars, as we call them, would never stop to think to themselves, 'Hang on, something doesn't add up here. This story conflicts with the one from last week?' No, they live only for the next 'Sensational revelation' and seem, conveniently, to forget the last one. Then they go on their forums, and using the lies and mis-information they have been spoon-fed by the cunning and conniving 'source,' they concoct their bizarre conspiracy theories about 'Team McCann,' and government cover-ups. You can't really blame them, most of them are the sort who skipped school, or if they did attend their local secondary modern, they would be the ones to hang around the bike sheds, having an illicit smoke, and threatening the first formers with a good hiding if they didn't hand over their pocket money. In other words not the sharpest knife in the drawer. No one with a good educational background, with a modicum of common sense would fall for these cheap tricks, surely?

Well, there's always ex-solicitor Tony Bennett. This is the same Anthony John Stuart Bennett that was Reprimaned at a Tribunal brought by the Law Society.

An application was heard at the Court Room 3rd Floor, Gate House, 1 Farringdon Street, London EC4M 7NS on the 9th September 2003. Quote from the Court papers: "(iv) by virtue of the aforementioned the Respondent had brought the profession into disrepute and is guilty of conduct unbefitting a solicitor."

A disgraced ex-cop and a disgraced ex-solicitor. They make a good couple, don't you think? But back to Mr Bennett. OK, so he gave solicitors a bad name, but he must have been pretty bright to have become one in the first place, yes?

You would like to think so, but no. Unfortunately Tony has also written a book, 'What really happened to Madeleine McCann?: 60 reasons that suggest she wasn't abducted.' Chock full of the most sloppy research imaginable, Mr Bennett relies heavily on Mr Amaral's morbid tome, and uses it as a foundation for his own. When he runs out of ideas to borrow from 'The truth of the lie' Mr Bennett then turns to the lower class forums mentioned elsewhere in our book, and copies great swathes of their more outlandish theories, and writes them up, and attempts to convince us they are true. They must be true, because they wouldn't lie to Tony, would they?! At no time did Mr Bennett himself make the slightest attempt to verify any of the so called 'reasons' written or copied into his own book, and that, we believe, will be his downfall.

But what do REAL policemen think? What is the professional opinion of REAL experts? Did she really die in the apartment, as Messrs Amaral and Bennett so desperatly want us to believe?

Let's take a look shall we?

Victims of the cops
Says JOHN O'CONNOR
Ex-Flying Squad Commander

DECENT people following the mysterious disappearance of Madeleine McCann wept at the anguish of parents Kate and Gerry and prayed for an end to their suffering.

They conducted themselves with such dignity and composure in public and did everything in their power to keep the case alive.

It is a tribute to their resourcefulness that this was a major story for more than a year — worldwide. Little Madeleine must be the best known child on this planet.

But the response of the Portuguese police was to make them arguidos and conduct a vicious sniping campaign by leaking apocryphal stories to the Portuguese media.

The tragedy of this investigation is that the police were woefully slow off the mark and wasted valuable time and resources in trying to find the answers within the family.

How completely wrong they were.

It was painfully obvious from day one that Madeleine had been taken by an intruder and probably by someone who had been watching the McCanns and their friends.

FBI Agent Analyzes McCann Case

http://abcnews.go.com/2020/Story?id=4766445&page=1

Brad Garrett Discusses Madeleine's Disappearance with ABC's Elizabeth Vargas

By SUSAN MILLER
May 2, 2008

"20/20" co-anchor Elizabeth Vargas recently spoke with former FBI Special Agent and profiler Brad Garrett, an ABC News consultant, who discussed the details surrounding the disappearance of Madeleine McCann.

Reports said the Portuguese police arrived on the scene soon after Madeleine vanished, and left soon after, a fact Garrett called "unusual." Garrett, who has worked on several high-profile missing persons cases, including that of Chandra Levy in Washington, D.C., said investigators would typically form a "command post right inside the resort. You start collecting information, and everything comes back to a lead detective in a room, and that's how you go through the information. You prioritize what needs to be done. ... You want to be right in the middle of the action so you can make snap decisions as to what should be done at any given time."

Garrett added, "You put people in places like airports, ports for boats" and you secure the scene as well as the resort so that everyone coming in and out is vetted.

From his experience, Garrett said that typically, in an investigation like this, the police would obtain and review surveillance tapes from the resort and any surrounding areas. And police would generally have a set team of law enforcement in place from the very beginning.

"Every case that I've worked like this you usually have a case agent, an FBI case agent and a lead detective," he said. "They sit right next to each other, and they work from that location, and everything comes back to them to make decisions on what should be done."

It would have been helpful in the McCann case, Garrett said, to know which cabs arrived at the resort. Additionally, he said police should have spoken with the entire staff at the resort to figure out if there were any people working there who had a history with missing children. "People get hired and there's limited background done on them," he said.

At times, the McCanns expressed little emotion during public appearances related to the case. Reports emerged that they had been advised by law enforcement not to break down in public. Garrett confirmed that "there is a belief in the world of criminal profiling that by keeping a very steady pace and talking in an authoritative but not condescending manner that you're sending a message out" to whoever may have abducted the child.

"You want to keep calm," he said. "The last thing you want is for them to get excited. They see this hysteria, that's one side of it. The other is some of these guys get kicks out of watching parents suffer on camera."

Garrett said Madeleine could have been taken by someone looking to adopt a blond 4-year-old attractive child. In these types of scenarios, "they actually have somebody go out and look for the child," Garrett said. Adoptive parents also might go to an agency that's unscrupulous and abducts children, he said.

But how could someone take Madeleine from her room without anyone hearing her cry or making noise?

Garrett said there are a few explanations. The McCanns have said that their children sleep quite soundly and that the twins apparently slept through the abduction. They even slept through the police coming into the room, the couple said.

Another theory?

Madeleine might have known her abductor, Garrett said. Somebody might have independently befriended her, possibly someone who works at the resort, he said.

Maddie's parents are INNOCENT

Lord Stevens

http://www.newsoftheworld.co.uk/news/article 10142.ece

THERE'S absolutely no chance that the parents of Madeleine McCann would be charged with her murder in this country. It would be an outrageous miscarriage of justice if they were. I don't say that from any feelings of sympathy for Kate and Gerry McCann, but from examining the facts of the case — or rather, the total LACK of them.

I've been a detective at the most senior level for 30 years and have never seen such a witch-hunt, or one based on such flimsy evidence. Again, I don't say this from believing in the McCanns' innocence or their guilt. I simply don't know either way. But from the evidence I have read I don't think they did it. Unless the Portuguese police have something else, it doesn't make sense. The couple don't fit the profile and their opportunity was limited.

Throughout my career I have based my conclusions on hard evidence—and here there isn't any. Sadly, I have to admit that is **because of the sheer inadequacy of the police investigation** that began when little Madeleine disappeared on the night of May 3. Among the many things the Portuguese police SHOULD have done that night, but didn't, was treat the McCanns as the prime suspects. Tragedy. That's what I'd have done. It's a matter of statistical fact that three out of four child murders are committed by the parents. So their behaviour, movements, what they said, how they said it, what they did, who they were with, should have been instantly put under the police microscope. They should have been sympathetically but relentlessly grilled again and again about what had happened that night. They weren't. That police error has become their tragedy now, because if they had been properly investigated back then they may well have been cleared. And thus free now to concentrate on the hunt to find their missing four-year-old, rather than somehow proving their innocence.

Hand-in-glove with treating the McCanns as suspects, the entire apartment and its environs should have been totally sealed off and barred to anyone but specially-trained police and forensic scientists who would have checked every millimetre of it for evidence. It wasn't.

Police don't call the time after a crime, particularly one against children, the Golden Hour for nothing. In fact, I always insist it's a Golden Day — the time when forensic evidence is most fresh and easy to detect, when memories are most sharp, when lies and alibis are most vulnerable. At its most basic, a bloodstain is easiest to see when it's still wet. Instead, Kate and Gerry McCann were just treated as grieving parents. Nicer for them, but no use in solving a crime they may have been involved in. And the possible murder scene was treated as a glorified meeting-room to organise a search for a missing child, instead of the potential treasure trove of clues it actually was. **To any experienced British detective, it is incomprehensible.**

I spent ten years heading Britain's Psychological Offender Profiling Committee for the Home Office. It was set up after the so-called Railway Murders, in which monster John Francis Duffy killed two women and stalked and raped four others close to London train stations. I worked alongside other very senior detectives, top civil servants and psychological profilers like Professor David Canter — who this week appeared on a TV programme about Madeleine's disappearance.

And I instinctively found myself agreeing when my friend Prof Canter concluded: **"I feel abduction is the most likely possibility."** In other words, the McCanns were not involved. Everything I've learned about the couple tells me their profile simply doesn't fit as killers of their own child. They've been criticised for being too controlled in their dealings with the media. It doesn't surprise me at all. They're both highly professional medics, one a surgeon the other a GP. They're trained and experienced in dealing with crises — and professionals react to crises with calm. Of course, anyone can get caught in horrendous circumstances and in panic try to lie their way out of it. But my experience has shown those lies, particularly elaborate and choreographed deceit as this would have to be, can rarely be maintained before cracks start to show. And particularly so when the suspects choose to place themselves under the intense, unprecedented scrutiny the McCanns have faced. But that's just my opinion, informed and based on considerable experience as it is.

Meanwhile, **the police investigation that started so disastrously has turned to farce.** Every apparent stream of evidence has been either missed, fatally compromised or is simply ludicrous. For instance, Mrs McCann being allowed to hang on to Madeleine's favourite toy CuddleCat. Consoling for her, of course, but that's not the point — it had gone to bed with Madeleine, been taken from her and placed on a high shelf, presumably by the abductor. CuddleCat was therefore vital evidence. Even a rookie detective should know it was highly likely an abductor's DNA would be on it. But it was left for Mrs McCann to clutch, her other children to play with and spread Madeleine's DNA around.

Then there was the suggestion the McCanns somehow smuggled their daughter's body away in a car they hired 25 days after her disappearance.

Where did they hide the remains in that time? How did they do this when their every move, at their encouragement, was under the media spotlight? There's also a very unpleasant aspect to face. What state, unless it had been in a deep freeze, would the body have been in? I'm afraid very gruesome indeed, probably with considerable leakage of bodily fluids and sloughing off of body cells. The smell alone would have been appalling and would linger endlessly in any enclosed space like a car. I'm bewildered by reports leaked by the Portuguese police that tiny traces have been found in the vehicle. My experience says it would probably be a great deal. If not, then anything found should be treated with extreme caution. In Britain, forensic evidence alone rarely solves cases. When it does, such as in rape cases, it hits the headlines because of its infrequency. But even then it's usually in support of more conventional evidence. None of the so-called forensic finds being boasted of in Portugal sound either likely, admissible or even possible to me. **Evidence from cadaver dogs, for instance, could not be used to bring about a conviction here.** Generally they are regarded as being **at best 80 per cent reliable.** And so it has gone on. The police haven't even found poor Madeleine's body — though that doesn't surprise me when you know rubbish bins in that small Portuguese seaside town weren't even searched in the week of her disappearance, before the contents were dumped in a landfill site.

To me, there is only one possible conclusion. **There is so far not a single shred of evidence that justifies charges against the McCanns.** But the worst thing is that, while the Portuguese police continue their single-minded determination to nail them, they ignore other lines of inquiry. And, worst of all, they are failing to carry on the hunt to try to find Madeleine alive.

But it comes to something, don't you think, when even the Portuguese authorities don't believe Mr amaral's account, that she died in the apartment. In fact, Portuguese prosecutors, in their final report, ridiculed detectives investigating Madeleine McCann's disappearance for uncovering "very little" conclusive evidence about the child's fate, the newly released files have revealed.

The damning report, made public as part of the massive dossier of evidence assembled over more than 14 months, **even compared local investigators unfavourably with Hercule Poirot and Sherlock Holmes.**

Written by public prosecutors in Portimao and dated July 21 – the day the case was officially shelved – the document said the investigation had not been able to find any proof which would allow **"the formulation of any lucid, sensible, serious and honest conclusion"** about the circumstances of how Madeleine went missing. It continued: "This includes the most dramatic thing, ascertaining whether she is still alive or dead, or even which seems the most probable."

"The investigators are fully conscious that their work is not exempt from imperfections. They worked with an enormous margin of error and they achieved very little in terms of conclusive results, especially about the fate of the unfortunate child.

"This is not, unfortunately, a detective novel, a crime scenario fit for the investigative efforts of a Sherlock Holmes or Hercule Poirot, guided by the illusion that the forces of law and justice can always re-establish order."

The 58-page report written by public prosecutors Jose de Magalhaes e Menezes and Joao Melchior Gomes was contained in the final volume of the files released to the media.

Prosecutors on McCanns' actions and their treatment by police.

The prosecutors' report said Madeleine's parents **did not "act with intent"** in leaving their children alone in their holiday apartment the night the child went missing.

"They could not predict that in the resort they chose to spend their holidays they could place the life of any of their children in danger."

They also noted that: "We must also recognise that the parents are paying a heavy penalty — the disappearance of Madeleine — for their carelessness in monitoring and protecting their children.

It went on: "While it is a fact that Madeleine disappeared, the circumstances of how this happened is not known.

"Even if, as a hypothesis, that Gerald and Kate could have been responsible for the death of the child, it would always be left to explain how, where, when, with what means, with whose help they disposed of the body."

It highlighted their "normal behaviour adopted before and after the disappearance."

It said: **"In reality, none of the suspicions which led to them being made arguidos came to be confirmed later."**

Let us examine this key phrase again.

The document said the investigation had not been able to find any proof which would allow **"the formulation of any lucid, sensible, serious and honest conclusion"**

Any lucid, sensible, serious and honest conclusion. So, dear reader, what then of Mr Amaral and Mr Bennett, and their postulation that Madeleine probably died in the apartment? May we suggest that, though we cannot be sure wether Madeleine is dead or alive at this moment in time, we CAN be as sure as is reasonably possible that she did NOT die in the apartment.

7. Now we want the TRUTH.

We would like to start this stage of our book with the following press editorial.

Opinion article by Henrique Monteiro, chief editor of Expresso:

http://www.liverpoolecho.co.uk/views/liverpool-columnists/paddy-shennan/2008/08/06/sadly-beauty-is-in-the-eye-of-the-voter-100252-21477766/

The judicial secrecy and the press lies.

Who lied in the Maddie case? The answer lies in what is told by former inspector Gonçalo Amaral. All the fantastic and never proved theories that a certain press has spread are in his book. And they remain without any evidence to sustain them.

Gonçalo Amaral must be a man who is full of himself. **He was responsible for a calamitous investigation** in the

Maddie case, but according to the balance that he does, everyone is to blame except for him.

According to Gonçalo, the blame lies with the fact that the McCanns apartment was not preserved, with the British police that did not fully cooperate, with the journalists that stood in the way, with Her Majesty's government that pressured, with the Portuguese government that let itself be pressured, with the prosecutors, with the PJ's directors, with the conspiracy of the powerful and if he is allowed to continue unloading it will hit the CIA, the Masonry, Opus Dei, the Trilateral, Bildeberg and the Pope, the usual suspects of the conspiracy theories that circulate on the internet.

The same inspector must not be inhibited (not to mention being ashamed), because after the suspicions that befall him due to the conduction of the Joana case (another missing girl, whose mother, who was condemned over her death, accuses the PJ of torturing her) and the disaster of the Maddie case, he pretends to be a national hero and the holder of the truth, against everything and against everyone, **and he maintains an absurd theory that does not resist a minimally structured analysis.**

Amaral probably didn't think about the fact that it does not become him to talk and to write in detail about a process which despite having been widely abused is still under judicial secrecy, either. Or that it does not become him to be a judge in his own cause.

But the most interesting about the former inspector's book is that we get to know where the famous lies from the media that everyone talked about, came from. Finally, we can verify that the most unbelievable theories came out of that illuminated brain. And that certain newspapers, lacking a better option, published them without contradicting, without investigating, without logics and without evidence.

But Gonçalo continues to state his conviction that Maddie died in the apartment. He must have inherited from medieval justice, **this notion of conviction without evidence;** or from Alice, by Carroll, the idea that first the criminals head is cut off and then the trial is done; or from The Foreigner, by Camus, the fixation in the importance of the criminals facies or the fact whether one does or does not cry in front of death.

The lawful state bases itself on evidence, beyond doubt. The notion that innocence prevails over guilt when there is no evidence to the contrary is what separates civilization from barbarism.

Unfortunately, there are remains of barbarism among us. Until very recently, it headed the PJ in Portimão. I hope he was the last one.

An interesting observation, don't you think, coming as it does, not from the British press, but one of the more respected papers in Mr Amaral's own country, where you would think he would have more support. What was the first line again, **Who lied in the Maddie case?** We hope by now you share our opinion that the truth most certainly will NOT be found in either Mr Amaral or Mr Bennett's literary non-masterpieces. The REAL truth, to quote a famous T.V. series IS out there. A helpless, innocent little girl is still missing, her parents torn with grief and worry, and all Mr Amaral can worry about is where and how his next euro can be wrung from this case. We think it is time Mr Amaral was put under the spotlight, and made to answer some searching questions about his handling of the case. This is now the time to come to the crux of this book, the questions we want Mr Amaral to answer. In fact, we DEMAND he be forced to answer them, under the glare of a full and open public enquiry. HE may not give a damn about what happened to Madeleine, but WE do, and we will not rest, will not cease, nor be silent, until we get the answers to these questions.

8. QUESTIONS WE DEMAND ANSWERS TO.

1 You had a call from an English couple in deep distress, their daughter had vanished, the whole of PDL (except for Robert Murat) was out searching for her. Have you confirmed Robert Murat was not involved in the search??

Source, PJ files

On that very night, the surroundings of the apartment, and Vila da Luz itself, were intensely searched through, both by the GNR members and by members of the public. Despite the exhaustive and methodical investigation into MURAT and the persons close to him, no elements whatsoever were collected to relate him to the crime that was under investigation, and it should be noted that contrary to what witnesses within the group stated concerning his hypothetical participation in the searches on the night of the disappearance, other witnesses (like SILVIA BAPTISTA and elements of the GNR) asserted that they had not seen him during those diligences.

2. How long after you knew that Madeleine had disappeared did you decide this was a case of a child wandering off and then instruct your men to go home and return the next morning if needed?
3. Do you always assume that small children going missing from their beds in the evenings have gone wandering off on their own in the dark?
4. How long did you sleep knowing that a small child was missing from her bed?

On 2nd June, 2007, Richard Edwards reported in the Telegraph that four weeks after Madeleine went missing, the police investigation into her disappearance still appears to be suffering from the "basic errors" made in first few hours.

Richard Edwards points out that the Police were at the scene **quickly but officers played down suggestions that Madeleine had been abducted and believed she had just wandered off.** The crime scene in and around the hotel was not taped off, ruining prospects of obtaining vital forensic evidence.

FBI Agent Analyzes McCann Case

http://abcnews.go.com/2020/Story?id=4766445&page=1

Brad Garrett Discusses Madeleine's Disappearance with ABC's Elizabeth Vargas

Reports said the Portuguese police arrived on the scene soon after Madeleine vanished, **and left soon after,** a fact Garrett called "unusual."

---

5. What time did the first call come in to which the GNR responded?
6. What time did the GNR request the PJ to come to the apartment?

http://en.wikipedia.org/wiki/Disappearance_of_Madeleine_McCann#cite_note-abducted-16

At around **22:00,** Kate returned to check on the children and found Madeleine's bed empty and the bedroom window open. Kate said that the police were called **within 10 minutes** of finding her daughter gone. Gerry said it was one of their friends who alerted the resort manager and the police.The GNR's_spokesman, Lieutenant Colonel Costa Cabral, said that the first call to the police (PJ) was at **23:50.**

On 5ᵗʰ May, 2007, Mr McCann's sister Philomena, on the BBC news website, criticised the Portuguese police for initially "playing down" their response to the disappearance.

She had been in phone contact with her brother that day.

Speaking from her home in Glasgow on the 5th, she said: "He thinks it's just too little, too late.

"It was hours before the local police turned up and we're talking two bobbies that totally downplayed the incident and said that Maddie had maybe just wandered off.

---

7. Did you immediately dispatch teams of your men and the GNR to do preliminary searches?

A reporter from the Telegraph said that officers failed to make early house-to-house inquiries when potential witnesses were still likely to be in the resort. Their reporter, Richard Edwards says that only on the Saturday, **more than 48 hours later,** did they start searching some local apartments and a full list of guests was obtained on Sunday. It wasn't untill **60 hours** after Madeleine disappeared that staff at Mark Warner's complex were questioned. There are still people who were in the same apartment block as Mr and Mrs McCann who have never been questioned. **Empty properties yards from where the child was taken have never been searched**.

---

8. Is it true that you never attended the scene yourself on the night Madeleine was abducted, but coordinated the investigation by phone? Where exactly did you coordinate this investigation from?
9. How was it possible to coordinate the search for a missing toddler over the telephone?
10. Did it not occur to you that there was a serious situation here and perhaps you had better get to the scene, take control and coordinate it properly?

11. On the night of May 3, 2007 how much had you had to drink after 18:00 hours?
12. If you had chosen to drive to Praia da Luz when the call for help was made on May 3, 2007 would you have been breaking the law?
13. Is that in fact one of the reasons you chose to coordinate from home?

Source.

"The truth of the lie."

By Goncalo Amaral.

"The first 72 hours On that night, 3rd of May of 2007, I decided to have dinner in the beer - river branch Carvi, good in the center of Portimão, before beginning the travel of return to house. A year since was finding me in that city, directing the department of criminal investigation of the Judicial Police officer. In 1982, with twenty three years of age, in the beginning of my investigator's run, the Portimão had moved and there connected knowledge with a charismatic figure of that land, ex-leader camarário and athletic, simple person and dinâ - mica, my friendly Manuel John. Much helped the elements of the PJ that for there were moving in service. While autarca was the impulsionador of the installation, in the city, of a department of the Judicial Police officer. It was with this fascinating person and good con - tador of histories that again I decided to share the sacred moment of the meal. For you realize between them of the coast vicentina and the shrimp of the rock, we were speaking about several problems of the socie - dade Portuguese.

For twenty four hours, already when of I left on the house way, I receive the piece of news that the Republican National Police had comu - when the disappearance of a 4-year-old English girl of age, of the interior of an apartment was pecked to the squad service, while the parents had dinner to a hundred of meters. The child was meeting on holidays with the family in the Town of Luz, in Lakes.

---

14. Why did you expect distraught parents to do YOUR job and secure a crime scene?
15. In view that it was YOUR obligation and YOUR job to see that a crime scene is properly secured, why did YOU allow so many people to contaminate it?

Source. PJ files.

It should be emphasized that the entire apartment had been searched and rummaged by an undetermined number of people, **with the contamination that it brings** and the difficulty that it raises for the collection of residues.

Inspector Chief Tavares de Almeida forgets his holiday because of the case. All Portuguese forces were now aware of the crime as well as Interpol. Searches start. The apartment had been **contaminated by friends of the couple,** employees from the resort, GNR officers and their dogs and other unknown people.

---

16. Why did no one order the flat to be cleared of all people that should not be there and then order that it be cordoned off IMMEDIATELY?
17. Why did you not consider getting the apartment properly examined by properly trained forensics teams IMMEDIATELY?

Mark Williams-Thomas, a former Surrey detective and now a leading child protection expert, in an interview said: **"I am staggered that it has taken so long."**

"The police **should have sealed the apartment immediately,** on day one and then conducted **a thorough forensic examination**- this would have taken days and would have involved analysis for fluids and fibres and involved stripping the apartment bare.

"Even if this proves not to be significant, it should have been discovered in the first few days and eliminated. This shows just how inept the Portuguese police were at carrying out the initial forensics tests.

"It's astounding that it has taken this long to bring in specialist help. It makes a mockery of the Portuguese investigation."

---

18. Why did you leave this couple to do their own searching, while you stayed home in bed?

---

19. If you were home knowing that the crime scene was being contaminated, why then ask the parents why they allowed people into the apartment?

Source, Kate's diary.

SUNDAY, JUNE 17: Cherie Blair (then the Premier's wife) phoned to find out how we were.

We talked about everything in general, including about them leaving Number 10. She agreed as well to make a 20-second video clip for our broadcast on YouTube about Madeleine and children who have disappeared.

I also had the chance to speak to Tony (then Prime Minister) who told me that we weren't to hesitate to ask him if there was something he could do to help.

On Sky News tonight they suddenly said the Portuguese police had stated that the crime scene had been contaminated—because of us—and that fundamental evidence had been lost. **How dare they insinuate that our daughter's life could be put in danger because of us. Very angry. Very upset.**

I want to speak to someone now, but it's too late.

I changed my mind and I sent a text message to Ricardo (Portuguese police family liaison officer). I don't know if was a sensible idea but I feel really annoyed.

My darling little Madeleine, you know that we wouldn't do anything to put you in danger.

I love you very much and I am in agony right now.

I only have to hope that God helps us all now and that he brings you back to us, safe and sound, very soon.

I need you to come back Madeleine. You are the best thing in my life that has ever happened to me. XXXXX

I ended up feeling very upset. Everything overflowed. Terrified that we might not get Madeleine back. I simply cannot face that. Tears, despair, rage, helplessness. I spoke to Gerry, recited prayers. Please God, bring her back XX

I fell asleep after 1am.

---

20. Why did you initially refuse Scotland Yard experts help?

---

21. Were you not worried about the preservation of the crime scene and being on the spot to put in place the routine for when a child goes missing? Were you not worried about missing the 'Golden Hours?'
22. If you never attended the scene that night, how do you know that Kate sat on Madeleine's bed traumatised unable to move?
23. If you did not attend the crime scene and view the bed for yourself, how could you say that the bed did not look like it had been slept in? In any event the bed did look like it had been slept in by a small child and it looked like someone had turned the bedclothes back to lift her out. Why did you say that the bed was hardly touched then accuse Kate of sitting on it?

24. To an ordinary person, you are told a child has gone missing; the first thing you do is to search the place. Behind the sofa, in the wardrobe, behind the curtains. Why do you think this is odd? Why did YOU not stop them?

---

25. Why did you not organise a search for the child IMMEDIATELY?
26. Why did you not order an immediate fingertip search at first light outside from where Madeleine went missing, instructing people what to look for, cigarette butts, matches, etc and tell them how to gather and secure this evidence?
27. Why did the police not carry out door to door searches immediately Madeleine was reported missing believed abducted?
28. Why did you not set an operations centre up in Mark Warner and order the lock down of the complex?
29. Why did you not ask MW manager for a list of all staff and all people holidaying that night?
30. Why did you not order the organisation of the immediate interviewing of all MW staff and residents?

http://www.people.co.uk/news/news/tm_method=full%26objectID=20691904%26siteID=93463-name_page.html

10 August 2008

Dodgy trackers top a catalogue of police howlers
EXCLUSIVE DOGGED BY BLUNDERS
By Dean Rousewell

The bungles began almost as soon as Maddie was reported lost.

Bedding was not forensically tested for traces of an abductor.

Cops failed to seal off the flat in the hours after the disappearance.

No fingertip search of local streets was carried out at the time - **and house-to-house inquiries were not launched for 48 hours.**

Two days passed before police got a list of other holidaymakers at the complex - by which time many of them **had already flown home.**

---

31. Did you have a proper scene of crime room out of which to operate?

FBI Agent Analyzes McCann Case

http://abcnews.go.com/2020/Story?id=4766445&page=1

Garrett, who has worked on several high-profile missing persons cases, including that of Chandra Levy in Washington, D.C., said investigators would typically form a "command post right inside the resort. You start collecting information, and everything comes back to a lead detective in a room, and that's how you go through the information. You prioritize what needs to be done. ... You want to be right in the middle of the action so you can make snap decisions as to what should be done at any given time."

"Every case that I've worked like this you usually have a case agent, an FBI case agent and a lead detective," he said. "They sit right next to each other, and they work from that location, and everything comes back to them to make decisions on what should be done."

---

32. Have you taken DNA samples from all residents, all holiday makers and all staff present at MW on and shortly before May 3rd?

Numerous press reports at the time raised question marks over the forensic evidence as it was shown that the Portuguese police **had failed to take DNA samples** from people who helped in the initial stages of the search for Madeleine.

These profiles would have proved crucial in matching scene-of-crime evidence to those who were at the resort.

Speaking in one paper, one resident who had not been asked to give a sample said: 'I thought it was quite important for us to give DNA so that we could be ruled out if nothing else. There were lots of us helping look for the little girl that night and you would have thought our DNA would be all over the place.'

---

33. Why did you not order the Spanish borders with Portugal to be informed you had a missing child believed abducted and issue them with photographs and details?
34. Same with the Marina just short distance away, why did you not order the lock down of this Marina?
35. Why did you not inform authorities at the airport?
36. Why did it take you 24 hours after Madeleine went missing to alert all border controls?

http://www.people.co.uk/news/news/tm_method=full%26objectID=20691904%26siteID=93463-name_page.html

Border guards were only alerted about Maddie after 24 hours and coastguards were told nothing for 14 hours.

---

37. Why did you allow Mark Warner cleaning staff to come in and clean apartment 5a and then ask Kate McCann why the flat had been cleaned
38. Why did you allow MW staff to enter this flat, a crime scene, and remove vital evidence such as the child's bedding?
39. Is it a possibility that the evidence of cleaning you have asked Mrs McCann about could have been the evidence of cleaning left by the MW cleaners that you allowed to enter and clean a crime scene in the first few days after Madeleine disappeared?
40. Is it possible that the apartment was then cleaned again by those allowed to rent the apartment weeks after Madeleine went missing?

---

41. Did you at anytime think that the abductor could have been putting up a pretence and was helping in searching the flat?

_____

42. When the police finally did start searching, in what locations was Maddie searched for, how and in what manner?
43. Where were you during these searches, and what were you doing?
44. Why did you not organise an immediate 15K ring search centring on the area that Madeleine disappeared from?
45. How many flats have been searched in the MW complex and when were they searched?
46. When were the MW buildings searched? i.e. cellars, offices, backs of restaurants, empty apartments etc?
47. Did you organise an immediate search of all barns, gardens and cellars in the immediate vicinity?

_____

48. Is it true that finger prints were not lifted from this apartment until five days after Madeleine went missing?
49. Is it true that the first finger prints lifted from the apartment were not taken properly and had to be re taken?
50. Why didn't the forensics technician taking the finger prints from the shutter and the bedroom window dress appropriately in accordance with international guidelines for taking forensic evidence?
51. Why do you think it strange that Kate's fingerprints were on the window, but not the abductors? Are you

not aware that most criminals, with intent to break and enter, wear gloves?

From our forum

From the offset there were many blunders in the normal investigation of the Madeleine Mccann case.

However there were also the most amazing blunders on the forensic side of this investigation and in this particular investigation, the forensics and DNA were always going to prove highly significant.

One such blunder that sticks in my mind is, we all saw on our TV screens, a woman forensic technician taking finger prints from the one of the most contentious areas of the forensic investigation of this case....the bedroom window.

She was, dusting for finger prints:

- **It was amazing that we could see all this at all!**
- **This whole area should have been covered with a tent, to prevent further contamination!**
- **She had her unruly hair down which was blowing in the breeze!**
- **She had on only ONE glove and that was on her LEFT hand.**
- **She was applying the powder with the brush with her RIGHT UNGLOVED hand.**
- **Her overalls were not fastened.**
- **She did not have a mask on.**
- **She could have blown away a single hair with her breath, (apart from other contamination's)!**

- **Her case was on the BARE ground, allowing further matter to be carried inside the apartment.**
- **She did NOT have her correct footwear on, or even overshoes, thus allowing further contamination.**

She should have been correctly scene of crime suited and booted. She sould have been covered from head to toe in a proper suit, the only skin visible should have been the little left on her face.

I remember listen to the commentary of a *proper* forensic scientist talking about this as they were showing this clip of this woman taking these finger prints, he said that just about every single thing that one should NOT do, while taking these fingerprints, this person had done it, he also said, that if this was the shocking standards outside, where we could all see, he was extremely worried about what was going on with the harvesting of forensic evidence inside the apartment, where we could NOT see!

As far as he was concerned, this evidence would be contaminated and the universal code for gathering evidence in such cases had not been adhered to.

Remember also that this evidence was not even taken until day FIVE of the investigation and up until that point any Tom, Dick and Jose' could simply walk up to that window and touch it and look through it as it was not sealed off!

---

52. Considering how important the shutter was to this investigation, why was the shutter not taken away and stripped down for proper analysis?

_____

53. Is it true that proper forensic examination of this flat did not take place until Day 100 after Madeleine went missing?
54. When the McCann's moved out of this apartment, who else had access to it?
55. Was the flat cordoned off and kept locked and secured and was it guarded at all times by a police guard after the McCann's had moved out?
56. In your opinion could anyone have had sufficient time, motive and opportunity to plant evidence in that apartment?
57. Why did you allow apartment 5a to be used by numerous other holiday makers for 2 out of the three months since Madeleine disappeared?

Entries in the official files show that the apartment where Madeleine vanished was used by holiday-makers for nearly two months before police sealed it off as a permanent crime scene.

It lay empty for a month after Madeleine's disappearance, but was then available to tourists throughout the summer.

Apartment 5A in the Ocean Club resort was eventually cordoned off in August after sniffer dogs from the UK - trained to detect corpses and human remains - were brought in.

Details of all those who stayed in 5A after the McCanns were disclosed in an internal document written by Chief Inspector Vitor Matos to Goncalo Amaral, who was then leading the investigation.

It showed that the McCanns booked the flat from April 28 for a week, but moved out on the morning after Madeleine vanished on May 3 last year.

On June 12, a couple from Liverpool who were friends of the owner, retired teacher Ruth McCann - who is no relation to Kate and Gerry McCann - stayed in 5A for a week.

A family of four from Falkirk in Scotland stayed from June 28 to July 12, followed by a couple from New Barnet in Hertfordshire.

On July 19, a family of three from Leicester stayed for a week.

---

58. Why were the bins in Luz allowed to be emptied shortly after Madeleine went missing?
59. Has the waste tip where the rubbish from Praia da Luz is taken been searched thoroughly for any signs of Madeleine, or her pyjamas or anything else missing?

---

60. When did you order a list of all paedophiles known to be in the area at this time?

61. Did you get in touch with the German police and the Swiss police about two paedophiles known to be in Praia da Luz at the time of Madeleine McCann's disappearance?
62. Did you yourself question all known witnesses that night of May 3rd?
63. Did you ask your men to ask for all witnesses to come forward and make a list of them before they left the apartment that night to go home to bed?

---

64. Is it true that the witness Mrs Pamela Fenn said she heard *A* child crying and did NOT say she heard *Madeleine* crying?

(The following needs to be read carefully, and understood, because the PJ made a very great deal out of this witness and what she is supposed to have said.)

Source official PJ files.

On page 2412, is the interview with PAMELA FENN, who relates several details, of which, though not clarifying the facts, are elucidating. Pamela Fenn lives on the first floor of the residential block, above the apartment occupied by the McCANN family. She related that, on 1 May 2007, two days before the disappearance, at about 22h30, she heard a child crying, which by the sound was MADELEINE. The child continued weeping for one hour and 15 minutes, until the parent's arrival (she heard the door sounds), at about 23h45. This witness places in cause the allegation (by the parents) of the daily routine of visits every 30 minutes to check the children who had been left on their own.

However, this police statement was clearly undermined when Mrs Fenn, in a press interview, dismissed the police version, saying it was "absolute rubbish" she had made any such claims to police. Mrs Fenn said: "I didn't even know that family was in there."

Also see video clip, where Mrs Fenn denies making said statement.

http://uk.youtube.com/watch?v=VTrFb-0zLuY

The following is an explanation of what Mrs Fenn could have heard.

From witness statements of Bridget O'Donnel and Jes Wilkins

They booked a large table every night in the Tapas. We called them "the Doctors". **Sometimes we would sit out on our balcony and their laughter would float up around us.** One man was the joker. He had a loud Glaswegian accent. He was Gerry McCann. He played tennis with Jes.

One morning, I saw Gerry and his wife Kate on their balcony, chatting to their friends on the path below. Privately I was glad we didn't get their apartment. It was on a corner by the road and people could see in. They were exposed.

My phone rang as our food arrived; our baby had woken up. I walked the round trip to collect him from the kiddie club, then back to the restaurant. **He kept crying**

and eventually we left our meal unfinished and walked back again to the club to fetch our sleeping daughter. Jes carried her home in a blanket. The next night we stayed in. It was Thursday, May 3.

Our baby would not sleep and at about 8.30pm, Jes took him out for a walk in the buggy to settle him. Gerry was on his way back from checking on his children and the two men stopped to have a chat. They talked about daughters, fathers, families. Gerry was relaxed and friendly. They discussed the babysitting dilemmas at the resort and Gerry said that he and Kate would have stayed in too, if they had not been on holiday in a group. Jes returned to our apartment just before 9.30pm.

Bridget O'Donnel and Jes Wilkins were staying very close to the McCanns on an upper floor, in fact Bridget says she remembers looking down on the McCanns apartment from her balcony and **'LISTENING' to the 'doctors, (as they became known) laughing and joking'.**

Bridget and Jes gave a statement to the police in which **they stated that their child had not been very well,** and had **been crying for a couple of nights,** non stop and to pacify the child, Jes had taken the child out for a walk in the buggy.

In other words, Mrs Fenn could have heard Bridget and Jes's baby, and NOT Madeleine.

---

65. Did you think of asking the parents to ask the twins if they saw something? (Even though they were very

small and asleep and you probably would not get a coherent logical answer?)

66. Mr McCann pointed out to you he thought it was odd that the twins remained asleep during all the commotion, did you not think of getting the twins tested and physically examined by a doctor immediately as he suggested?

The parents are on record as stating the twins slept on like logs, just as they always did at home, though at the time they felt doubt creeping into their minds – had they been sedated by an abductor? – that they should be quite so comatose. The Ocean Club gave them another apartment, but the McCanns did not want to be alone, so the twins were taken to the Paynes' apartment, and Kate and Gerry went there later too, to try to rest.

---

67. Did you not think to come and help this couple who were alone in a foreign country unable to speak the language, alone panicking and petrified?

---

68. Why do you consider it strange that a member of the family contacted Sky News the following morning?
69. Why did you inform the press that the parents contacted Sky News BEFORE calling the police?
70. Did you consider cultural differences? Did you try to understand that publicity and advertising that a child has disappeared, using the media is how things are handled in Britain??

It should be pointed out, in terms of the media knowledge and divulgation, that witness RACHEL MAMPILLY, at around 2 a.m. on the morning of the 4th, assumes to have contacted the official British television BBC, through someone that she knew, reporting the disappearance and asking for it to be broadcast. First thing in the morning on 4 May, and already within the framework of heavy media coverage, an interview of the entire group took place, pages 34-83, interrogations which were repeated later.

In an article from the Times, dated Dec 16th, 2007, it is pointed out that it was Matthew Oldfield who went down to the 24-hour reception at the bottom of the hill to raise the alarm. The call to the police went in at 10.15. They arrived 55 minutes later. It is widely believed among the Portuguese media, and perhaps the police too, even now, that the McCanns called Sky News before they called the police. For the record, **Sky News picked up the story from GMTV breakfast television, at around 7.30am the following day.**

---

71. Why did you not order an immediate circulation of this child's picture, so people knew who they were looking for?
72. Why did you not issue a public appeal?
73. Do you as a serving detective, not know the European drill for a missing child believed abducted? Where cir-

culating a photo to the media is considered of **VITAL** importance?

74. Were you aware of the 'Child Rescue Alert System' which has been employed across Europe since 2007? Which was actually in force at the time Madeleine McCann went missing?

75. If you did know of this drill, why did you not put the Bullet Point list into operation immediately?

- Description of the child
- Scanned photo of the child
- Details of location and nature of the offence
- Description of the offender(s)
- CCTV/photo of the offender(s)
- Details of vehicle used

http://www.npia.police.uk/en/10239.htm

Child Rescue Alert

Child Rescue Alert is a system that was launched as a UK initiative to save abducted children from being murdered.

Introduction

The system works by seeking the assistance of the public where a child has been abducted and is feared to be in danger. Its intention is to raise awareness via the media that a child has been taken, so the public look out for the child, the abductor(s) or any vehicle used in the abduction and thereby engage their support.

Television and radio programmes are interrupted with immediate news flashes to ensure public vigilance and to encourage any information to be reported.

Child Rescue Alert Activation Criteria

There are four key criteria, all of which must be met before a Child Rescue Alert is issued:

- The child is under the age of 16-yrs-old
- There is reasonable belief that the child has been kidnapped or abducted
- There is reasonable belief that the child is in imminent danger of serious harm or death
- There is sufficient information available to enable the public to assist the police in locating the child

The key decision is whether to launch an alert at all as it is felt that overuse, or 'cry wolf' scenarios will destroy confidence in the system.

Authorisation to issue a Child Rescue Alert is required from a senior police officer. This officer may vary from force to force. The authorising officer will allow for a circulation of an alert to all the media outlets the individual force has agreements with.

Content of a Child Rescue Alert

A Child Rescue Alert may contain some or all of the following information:

- Description of the child
- Scanned photo of the child
- Details of location and nature of the offence

- Description of the offender(s)
- CCTV/photo of the offender(s)
- Details of vehicle used

Radio stations/TV stations (it varies from Force to Force) will broadcast this alert every 15 minutes for four hours. TV stations will use ticker tape style scrolling text at the bottom of the screen, directing the public to a page on their news text services or if it is a local transmission they will interrupt it and show a newsflash.

Members of the public will be encouraged to keep their eyes and ears open for anything that may assist the police in recovering the kidnapped child. If they spot anything they should call the police using the 999 system or the number that will be provided on screen or via the broadcast.

---

76. Did you check the CCTV cameras of people coming in and leaving the resort?

It was widely reported in the press that Portuguese police searching for Madeleine had **failed to seize local cctv footage** holding potentially vital clues to the abduction of the British toddler.

Authorities revealed that detectives have not asked for surveillance pictures of vehicles leaving Praia da Luz at the time of Madeleine's disappearance.

The press also reported criticism of the police's **failure to check motorway cameras for vehicles leaving Praia da Luz in** the immediate aftermath of Madeleine's kidnap. Euroscut, the company responsible for maintaining and administrating 80 miles of road between Lagos and Vila Real de Santo António, on the Spanish border, said the cameras act mostly as a deterrent and only record for around two hours a day.

However, they are always monitored in a control room.

Police did not contact the company in the hours after Madeleine's disappearance to alert them and have not approached them since to review material.

---

77. Concerning you professional career, how many missing child/abduction cases have you investigated?
78. What was the outcome of those cases?
79. Is there any controversy over those cases?

(See chapter on case histories; Joana Cipriano.)

---

80. Why did you think of bringing in sniffer dogs from the UK several months AFTER Madeleine went missing?

---

81. Are you aware of the FACT that two of the by-products of decomposition, putrescine and cadaverine, have been bottled and are commercially available as dog training aids?
82. Can this scent of death be produced in a laboratory for dog training purposes? Is this produced in any lab in

Portugal? Have you checked to see if anyone had recently purchased such a product? Have you checked out all those that have access to such product?

Until recently, so called sniffer dogs, those trained to search for, among other things, dead human bodies had to be indoctrinated with real human remains. But now, after analyzing and distilling the composition of decaying bodies, the Sigma Chemical Company of St. Louis, United States, produces scents specifically for the training of these dogs. Scents such as Pseudo Corpse, Pseudo Drowned Victim and Pseudo Distressed Body, the last for training dogs to find survivors of earthquakes and building colapses buried in rubble. Sigma is the only manufacturer of such scents, ranging in price from $1 a capsule to $25 an ampul.

---

83. Are you aware that these by-products are present in ALL decaying organic material, and also in human saliva?

Source The Independent 28.05.08.

A trained human cadaver dog will not signal a living person or an animal (except PIGS), but it will signal a recently deceased, putrefying or skeletonised human corpse. That suggests that the "bouquet of death" is discernible, but attempts to identify it have so far failed. Two of the by-products of decomposition, putrescine and cadaverine, have been bottled and are commercially available as dog training aids. But they are also present in **all** decaying organic material, **and in human saliva.**

84. Did you ever think that there may have been evidence left by the abductor/s that could have made the dogs react in this way?
85. Is it a possibility that such evidence could have been missed because you did not order the immediate securing of a crime scene?

---

86. Is it true that the blood found in the apartment 5a was found to be that of an Eastern European Male?
87. Is it possible that the blood indicated by the above was what the dogs reacted to?

http://www.independent.co.uk/news/world/europe/po-lice-no-breakthrough-in-search-for-madeleine-461916.html

Mr Ribeiro said a blood sample found at the McCanns' apartment had been sent to the UK to see if there was a match with the DNA database of British criminals but it was impossible to check the DNA sample against British expatriates living in Praia da Luz. He said: "That is not possible. The UK is the most advanced country with regard to databases. It has a much more complete database. But we cannot imagine making a comparison with all the British [in Praia da Luz]."

The blood test shows the sample probably came from a man from the "north-east European sub-group". That conclusion is only 72 per cent accurate, however, due to the poor condition of the sample because of its age and cleaning of the bedroom. The Forensic Science Service in

Birmingham is conducting further tests on the blood. A male guest is known to have injured himself while staying at the flat after Madeleine disappeared. That could explain why the blood was not found when Portuguese police searched the apartment after Madeleine's disappearance.

---

88. Is it possible that the scent the dogs reacted to could have been placed there by previous holidaying occupants of apartment 5a before the McCann's arrived?
89. If you felt so strongly that the parents were involved then why allow them to drive their car in for examination?

---

90. When the cars were lined up to be exposed to the sniffer dogs, why did you allow this procedure to take place in a public car park and not a scientifically controlled scene?
91. When these cars were lined up to be exposed to the dogs, why did you allow the McCann's hire car to remain highly identifiable by allowing the find Madeleine bright yellow stickers all over it?

Dog handler Martin Grimes own report

Ten vehicles were screened in **an underground multi storey car park at Portimao.** The vehicles, of which I did not know the owner details, were parked on an empty floor with 20-30 feet between each. The vehicle placement video recording and management of the process was conducted by the PJ. The EVRD was then tasked to search the area. **When passing a vehicle I now know**

to be hired and in the possession of the McCann family, the dog's behaviour changed substantially. This then produced an alert indication at the lower part of the drivers door where the dog was biting and barking. I recognise this behaviour as the dog indicating scent emitting from the inside of the vehicle through the seal around the door.

---

92. Is it true that the sniffer dogs walked past ALL cars in the line up, INCLUDING the McCann's hire car, indicating a NEGATIVE?
93. When the dogs walked past this vehicle and FAILED to indicate a positive reaction, why did you insist that they be brought back and walked around the car until they did indicate a positive?
94. Did you have any idea that the dogs may indicate a positive if they were repeatedly subjected to walking around this particular vehicle?

(We of the Justice for all the McCann family have all watched this video intently, many times. The dog was allowed, on average, 20-30 seconds at the first three cars. The dog ignored each car in turn. When they got to the McCann's hire car, CLEARLY IDENTIFIABLE by the 'Look for Madeleine' posters in each window, the dog AGAIN ignored the car. We watched as the dog was called back no less than FIVE TIMES to the car, clearly becoming more confused each time, before it finally reacted. This took nearly four and a half minutes, rather than the 20-30 seconds routine allowed for the previous cars.)

---

95. Bearing in mind the case of the Jersey Orphanage, where the dogs alerted to what later turned out to be a piece of coconut shell, how do you account for saying these dogs have never given a false sign in 200 cases?

---

96. Are you aware that in a similar case in the United States, a judge ruled out the evidence of sniffer dogs, saying they were 'no more reliable than the flip of a coin?'

The Times carried an article about the reliability of sniffer dogs, on Dec 16th, 2007, wherein they show the role of such dogs is normally intended to find a body or remains. Without any subsequent discovery the alerts amount to little more than an indication – or worse: in one recent case in Wisconsin a judge concluded that similarly trained dogs **were "no more reliable than the flip of a coin",** after hearing evidence that **they were wrong far more often than they were right.** The McCanns' lawyers are in touch with the defence lawyers in that case. The PJ had never attempted to obtain a "control sample" of Madeleine's DNA. That had been left to the McCanns, who had found traces of her saliva on the pillow of her bed at home in Rothley and provided that DNA sample to the Portuguese police.

---

97. Are you aware that one of the T-shirts the dog alerted to, was NOT Madeleine's, as you claimed, but in fact Sean's?

98. Is it true that your OWN officers have expressed doubts about the dogs handling, and the way they reacted to the McCann's hire car?

ANALYSIS REPORT OF THE FIRST 11 VOLUMES OF THE INQUIRY

(pages 1-3004)

Central Department of Criminal Investigation, February, 8th, 2008

From the screening of the videos, referred previously, done when the dogs were working, some doubts arise. We don't want and we can't take the place of the trainer, we only wish to alert, with this paragraph, to some facts, that according to us, need further clarification.

If the dog is trained to react when he detects what he is looking for, why, in most of the cases, we see the dog passing more than once by that place in an uninterested way, until he finally signals the place where he had already passed several times?

On one of the films, it's possible to see that "Eddie" sniffs Madeleine's cuddlecat, more than once, bites it, throws it into the air and only after the toy is hidden does he "mark" it (pag 2099). Whys didn't he signal it when he sniffs it on the first time?

Apart from all that was said about the dogs, we must also take into attention the results of the forensic analysis that was performed by the experts on the Scientific Police

Laboratory on the day immediately after the facts, and already mentioned where no vestige of blood was found.

---

99. If, as you recently claimed, Gerry buried Madeleine on the beach, why did the sniffer dogs not react to any of HIS clothes?
100. Did you even think of asking to have the dogs sniff his clothes?
101. Did you or any of your men have contact with dead or drowned human bodies prior to the sniffer dogs being brought to Portugal?

---

102. Is it true that ALL DNA evidence that has been found both inside the flat and the hire car is mitochondrial DNA which could have belonged to Madeleine, Amelie or Kate herself?
103. Is it true that you misinterpreted the DNA evidence from the FSS in Birmingham UK AND that from the Portuguese forensic science lab?
104. Why did you ignore the email from John Lowe of the FSS in Birmingham, three days BEFORE you made the McCanns arguidos, warning that the DNA samples were inconclusive? Why did you still proceeded to make The McCanns arguidos?
105. Why did someone then LIE to Gerry about the DNA in the hire car? As previously stated, the British FSS made it clear that the test results were inconclusive, and should in no way form part of any investigation. Yet four days later, someone lied to Gerry McCann, telling him the results were 100% positive. Is it usual to 'overstate the strength' of evidence in this way?

Portuguese police told Gerry McCann they had found in-criminating DNA from his missing daughter Madeleine FOUR days after British scientists warned them the fo-rensic evidence **could have come from anyone.**

Detectives were informed that 'evidence' gleaned from the family's holiday apartment and the boot of the hire car, crucially rented 25 days after the three year old van-ished, **was inconclusive**.

Yet they still made Gerry and his wife Kate officials suspects - and in an eight hour interrogation of Gerry, **stated as fact** that damning DNA had been found.

The extraordinaly statement was revealed as the mam-moth, 20,000 - page 'Madeleine File' detailing the 14 month Portuguese investigation was opened up to the public.

But it is an email from British scientist John Lowe, part of the major incidents team at the Birmingham-based Fo-rensic Science Service (FSS) on September 3, 2007, that provides a damning indictment of the controversial Por-tuguese investigation.

It is written to Detective Superintendent Stuart Prior, head of the British side of the investigation, and said that a sample taken from the McCanns' Renault Scenic hire car contained 15 out of 19 of the young girl's DNA com-ponents.

But Mr Lowe warned that this result - based on the con-troversial 'low copy' DNA analysis technique which uses very small samples - was 'too complex for meaningful interpretation or inclusion.'

The scientist wrote:' Let's look at the question that is being asked: ' Is there DNA from Madeleine on the swab?

'It would be very simple to say 'Yes' simply because of the number of components within the result that are also in her reference sample.

'What we need to consider, as scientists, is whether the match is genuine - because Madeleine has deposited DNA as a result of being in the car or whether Madeleine merely appears to match the result by chance.'

Mr Lowe then pointed out that components of the missing girl's DNA were not unique to her - in fact, some of them were present among FSS scientists, including himself.

He stressed that low copy analysis couldn't determine when or how the DNA was deposited, what body fluid it came from - and whether a crime had been committed.

He concluded : 'We cannot answer the question: is the match genuine, or is it a chance match.'

---

106. Have you traced, spoken to and checked out the professions and the occupants of those that rented the apartment after Madeleine went missing?

---

107. Is it true that pieces of paper which could have contained vital information in this investigation were just strewn about the PJ offices?

Numerous press reports tell how Paulo Rebelo, the second police chief in charge of the investigation, was furious at how it was left in disarray by his predecessor.

According to these reports, officers spent almost two weeks processing information left lying around on scraps of paper and following leads ignored by police working under Chief Inspector Goncalo Amaral.

Following Amaral's removal after he criticised British police, Rebelo, one of Portugal's national deputy police chiefs, reviewed the whole forensic investigation because of earlier procedural errors.

A police source quoted in a Portuguese newspaper said: "There was important material lying all over the place that hadn't been considered by investigators.

---

108. Is it true that the leaked report to the press of a boot print found inside the flat and on the bumper of the McCann's hire care was that of policeman belonging to the GNR?

http://www.people.co.uk/news/news/tm_method=full%26objectID=20691904%26siteID=93463-name_page.html

The catastrophic blunders continued after the shambles with the dogs.

Detectives spent hours poring over footprints found at the scene - which turned out to belong to policemen.

---

109. Is it normal in Portugal for someone you suspect in the case you are investigating, (Robert Murat) to be allowed to translate during key witness interviews?

It is now common knowledge how the first suspect in the Madeleine McCann case sat in on police interviews with some of the McCann's friends.

Robert Murat, 34 - who later became an arguido or official suspect - was allowed to act as a translator for police during crucial questioning of Kate, Gerry, and their companions.

It meant that he had an extraordinary insight into the investigation during the vital early days after Madeleine was abducted.

There were also fears that Mr Murat could have influenced the police's understanding of the statements.

One of the McCann's friends said "It beggars belief. It's absolutely outrageous that someone who a few days later is declared an arguido was aware of much of what initial witnesses said."

---

110. Why did you make them arguidos and then complain Kate would not answer questions, exercising

her right to remain silent under the arguido status that you yourself placed her under?

111. If you wanted Kate to answer your questions, why didn't you leave her a witness, explaining that under Portuguese law, witnesses are obliged by law to answer police questions?

---

112. Did Kate refuse to answer the questions after the alleged deal -2 year jail sentence?

113. Did she stop answering questions on the advice of her Portuguese lawyer?

114. And how given the secrecy order, did the fact that she had not answered these questions leak out from the investigation you were then heading?

Before putting the evidence to the couple in separate interviews, police had to declare them arguidos, assuring them the right to remain silent.

Before this point, they were simply witnesses. Under Portuguese law, a witness is bound to answer questions.

After Kate McCann was made an arguido, she declined to answer dozens of leading questions, such as what she saw and did on finding Madeleine gone; and why, when she raised the alarm, she left her two-year-old twins alone in the apartment.

She was fully within her rights not to respond, and according to the couple's spokesman **was advised by her lawyer not to.**

Only when asked by police if she realised she was jeopardising the investigation did she say: "yes, if that's what the investigation thinks."

---

115. Is it true that you asked for the secrecy order to be implemented in this case?
116. Is it true that the secrecy law need NOT have been evoked in this case?
117. Did you make Mr and Mrs McCann aware of the FACT that the secrecy law need not be applied in the investigation and search for their missing daughter?

Detectives could not issue information on the investigation due to strict Portuguese laws on "judicial secrecy". However the law **includes two exceptions, both of which apply in the case of Madeleine.**

It meant no direct appeal for help was made and police failed to give a clear description of Madeleine. There were no posters put up in the early days. **It was left to Madeleine's parents to describe what she was wearing on the night she disappeared.**

---

118. Is it true you made the McCann's arguidos "too hastily" just 8 days BEFORE the law was Due to change in Portugal?
119. Is it true that if you had waited to make the McCann's arguidos, you would have had to produce hard and fast evidence to do so? Is it true that you made the McCann's arguidos then because you had NO evidence to back your suspicions?

In a statement to many of the world's press representatives, Alipio Ribeiro, the Policia Judiciaria's national director, said he believes the decision to make the McCanns "arguidos" was taken too quickly and without thorough enough assessment.

"I think there perhaps should have been another assessment before the McCanns were made official suspects. I don't have any doubt about that ... there was a certain hastiness."

It also appears to back up criticisms voiced by the McCanns' lawyer in Portugal, Carlos Pinto de Abreu, who suggested that police had waged a smear campaign against the couple by rushing to make them suspects on September 8, 2007, just days before a new law would have made it impossible without firm evidence.

Portugal's Attorney General Fernando Pinto Monteiro has already admitted the McCanns, both 39, might not have been named arguidos after its introduction.

Mr Pinto de Abreu said: "Before September 15 last year you could be made an arguido without any suspicions or evidence against you.

"Now, to constitute someone as an arguido, it is necessary to have evidence in the file. That's why the national public prosecutor said that if this inquiry was launched now, maybe they would not have been made arguidos."

Asked whether he thought police acted deliberately as they knew the new law was coming in, he added: "I don't know if that's true, but yes, it's possible."

120. Who do you think as been leaking highly sensitive reports to the Portuguese press?
121. Why do you think they would leak these confidential reports to the press?
122. From where did Felicia Cabrita obtain all her information and is it true that her husband is your lawyer "Antonio Cabrita"?
123. Have you ever had lunch with Felicia Cabrita?
124. How in your opinion did Felicia Cabrita get hold of this 'extreme' information? Where did she get copies of witness testaments, witness names, addresses and telephone numbers?

The first public indication of police thinking came at the end of June when the magazine Sol published a story about the McCann group, casting doubts on their evidence and claiming they had undertaken a pact of silence. It was the first time the McCanns' friends had been named in public, but Sol's journalist Felicia Cabrita had their names and phone numbers and details from their witness statements. She had called them all, and at least one other witness, Jes Wilkins.

The information had been handed to Cabrita by the police – she says she acquired the material through good journalism, which in a sense it was – and her source is widely believed by her colleagues to have been the former head of the inquiry, Goncalo Amaral.

125. Is it true that you presided over a highly sensitive investigation where leaks from within this investiga-

tion were repeatedly used to blacken the characters of Kate and Gerry McCann?

126. Have you ever had any contact whatsoever, with Journalist Nacho Abad of Spanish television programme Ana Rosa Quintana?

http://www.itv.com/News/Articles/McCanns-angered-by-interview-leak-771901096.html

McCanns angered by interview leak

Published: Friday, 11 April 2008, 6:44AM

Kate and Gerry McCann claim they are the victims of a smear campaign as passages from their police interviews have been leaked.

While the McCanns were in Brussels supporting a child alert system, a Spanish television journalist made public parts of the interviews they gave immediately after Madeleine disappeared.

The McCanns are angry about the timing of the leak and described it as a "blatant" attempt to smear them.

They called for the Portuguese Justice Ministry to launch an internal investigation into the revelations, which would be a serious breach of the country's strict judicial secrecy laws.

The Policia Judiciaria interviews were leaked through journalist Nacho Abad, of Spanish television programme Ana Rosa Quintana.

127. Is it true that you dismissed many sightings, one in particular in Morocco, on the grounds that you assume Madeleine is dead and her parents are to blame?

From an interview with Amaral.

Q: Did you think from the beginning that this was not an abduction?

It is not normal that someone should insist and be determined that this was an abduction without considering another option. When a child disappears, one thinks she could have escaped and many other hypotheses. And the contradictions from all of them, lead one to think that something totally different happened. We worked on the abduction theory for two or three months and then we began to think about the theory of death.

Q: The police continued maintaining the abduction theory after considering that the girl was dead. Why?

The parents spoke of the abduction as a necessity. There was no security for the children because if there had been Maddie would not have disappeared. And the abduction theory was dropped when it was proved that it could not be based upon the open window.

---

128. Is it also true that a member of the hotel staff saw a man hiding in the bush near the McCanns apartment? And were there any footprints in the ground under that bush? If there were what was done about them? Were they investigated or ignored as many other

sightings and leads appeared to have been? And if this is true, why?

129. Why was the car park outside Madeleine's window not checked for tyre prints?

Police failed to investigate a previous suspected abduction attempt from Kate and Gerry McCann's holiday apartment, as disclosed in the official files.

A babysitter spotted a man lurking in the shadows outside apartment 5A while she was looking after a young girl inside.

But Portuguese police dismissed her account as 'irrelevant' and refused to investigate.

The failure turned out to be just one of a host of missed opportunities.

The case files showed that Margaret Hall, a babysitter at the Mark Warner resort, was interviewed by detectives working for the McCanns from the Spanish-based agency Metodo 3 last year.

They handed their report, marked 'Very Confidential', to the Portuguese police.

It said Miss Hall had been in apartment 5A with a young girl in September 2006 - eight months before Madeleine's disappearance - when she heard a noise outside.

She went to investigate, the statement said, adding: 'In a dark area she noticed something was moving and thought it was a rat.

'She was shocked when, on closer examination, she saw it was the brown shoe of a man. She shouted and the man came out of the darkness, activating movement-sensitive lights. He walked towards her, saying "No, no".'

---

130. Do you or anyone else that you know of have any financial assets which might suffer as a result of it becoming known that a child was abducted in the Algarve?
131. Did you hold any of those same conflicting interests when Joanna was abducted? (It is just a question not a statement)
132. In your opinion would a family oriented resort catering largely to British visitors suffer if it became known that a British child had been abducted by a human trafficking ring operating in the Algarve?
133. What date did your dog die and what contact did you have with the dog's cadaver?

---

134. According to rumours leaked about the McCanns from these sources "close to the PJ" the group were said to have drunk 14 bottles of wine on the night of May 3? The bill from the restaurant in your files indicates ONLY 2 bottle of wine and several bottles of non-alcoholic beverages (for the entire group) -- how would you explain that discrepancy?
135. And why was it leaked that they had drank more wine than you actually knew to be the case? If you were having dinner with a group of 9 people, would you have more than two bottles of wine on the table?

Police sources **suggested** the group generally drank daiquiris, martinis and beers before dinner, up to 14 bottles of wine with their meal, and almond liqueur afterwards.

However, local police officers who arrived at the complex on May 3 were reported in the Portuguese newspaper Correio da Manha as saying that the group "seemed to be normal" and were not drunk.

The group's waiter, Jose Baptista, added that they were "very sensible" about their drinking.

The official files contain the actual reciept for that night, showing only two bottles of wine were ordered.

---

136. Why did it take you over a week to instruct police to visit the only supermarket near the Ocean Club?

---

137. Due to the very close proximity (about 7 miles) that Joanna Cipriano went missing did you ever consider that there may be a connection between the disappearances of Joanna and Madeleine?
138. How would you have handled a connection between these two missing children if it had emerged?

---

139. How often did you keep Mr & Mrs McCann updated on the progress of the search for their daughter?

Desperate Kate McCann's heartbreak letter to police: 'Please end my torture'

Kate McCann sent the policeman heading the Madeleine inquiry a heart-rending letter pleading for news - and he cruelly snubbed her.

She said: "I am appealing to you to as a fellow human being to work with us and remember that we are Madeleine's parents and have needs.

"Madeleine is the most precious thing in our life. The lack of information is torture."

As she begs to be allowed to hear of any developments in the hunt for her missing daughter, she hints at the inhumanity of keeping her and Gerry in the dark.

An emotional Kate wrote: "As her mother, the pain and anxiety I feel for her is indescribable and the feeling of helplessness overwhelming.

"Even if we could have a little bit of information in the broadest of terms it would help.

"Lack of communication and a void of information, particularly as the parents of a missing child, is torture."

140. Why did you tell the McCann's not to speak to the Spanish journalist who claimed he knew of a French paedophile who was on his way to Portugal for his next victim? Especially as you were informed that there was paedophile activity in the area?

141. Did you ever return alone to inspect apartment 5a during the 3 months after Madeleine disappeared?

142. Regarding the other arguido 'Robert Murat'. Police say they completely searched the villa, but detectives spent less than a full day collecting material and then allowed the family to return, leading some to question how thorough they actually were. It takes days to complete a thorough forensic search, so how thorough was this search and did it follow international guidelines for correct forensic procedure?

---

143. Who was this mysterious witness you were on the brink of producing, just prior to being removed from the case?

144. Why was this witness' details not passed on to the new head of the investigation, if his testimony you considered to be most important?

Text: Carlos Tomas
July 07, 2008

When he was discharged, the former investigator of the Maddie Case was preparing to hear an Irishman, who was considered to be a very relevant witness. But the present investigators don't give him credibility

The statements from the Irish citizen who is considered to be a key witness in the Maddie case by Gonçalo Amaral, the man who lead the entire investigation, were not considered to be relevant by the investigators from the Polícia Judiciária who presently hold the process.

During the two depositions, both informal, the Irishman who is only known as "Smith" said that he saw the father of Madeleine McCann, Gerry, leaving the apartment in Praia da Luz, Lagos, Algarve, carrying a child on the day that the little girl disappeared. This, during the period of time between 6 and 10 p.m., precisely when Maddie disappeared.

"He was one of the witnesses that should be questioned within the rogatory letter that was sent to England. But, due to the fact that he is an Irish citizen, the authorities in Leicester, England, failed to contact him. The diligence was not deemed relevant, given the fact that he was informally heard at the beginning of the process and his depositions were highly contradictory", a senior officer who is connected to the investigations revealed to 24horas.

The same source specified: "First he said that he saw Maddie's father leaving the apartment carrying a child. **But during a second hearing he said he was not certain that it was Gerry who carried the child. He even said he could not assert whether said person was actually carrying a human being. This type of witness is not admissible in court and they do not deserve credibility".**

It is now up to prosecutor Magalhães e Meneses, who is analysing the process, to decide whether it is necessary to carry out further diligences, namely whether the hearing of the Irish citizen is necessary or not to reach a decision about the case, which apparently is to be archived concerning the suspicions of concealment of a cadaver and possible homicide that are pending on the McCanns.

145. Is it true that there was no communication whatso-
     ever between yourself and the new head of case? Is
     this normal behaviour, and can you explain this?

Amaral interview to Expresso 04.07.08.

Interviewer:
After leaving the investigation, did you ever speak
with your successor, Paulo Rebelo?

GA Answers:
No. It is an interesting question to consider. If they
removed me for the barbarity of speaking to the press,
and not for incompetence, it would be normal to be con-
sulted. But this never happened.

146. Why are you so adamant that Madeleine died in the
     apartment, yet are totally unable to explain why, with
     not one shred of evidence to back this 'hunch' up?

147. You recently claimed to believe that Gerry buried her
     on the beach. Why then, when Martin Grimes took
     the sniffer dogs to the beach, did they fail to react?
148. Are you aware that there are packs of stray dogs
     roaming the area? Is it not most likely that these dogs
     would have smelt a dead body and dug it up from the
     beach, assuming holiday makers digging sandcastles
     had already not done so?

149. How likely is it that Gerry could have returned twenty six days later, disinterred the body, and moved it to a new burial place, under the full glare of the world's media, without being spotted?

The ex Director of the Criminal Investigation department of the Police in Portimao, Gonçalo Amaral, who head the team searching for Madeleine McCann, has given an interview in today's El Mundo newspaper. The man who was sacked after making the parents suspects in the case **claims that Gerry McCann hid Madeleine's body on the beach,** and that the child died from an accident, claiming she could have fallen off the sofa or there could have been an overdose of Capel (sic: Calpol), a sleeping drug.

August 2007

OPERATION TASK CANINE SEARCH REPORT
Official report submitted by martin grimes, 'sniffer' dog handler.

I am a 'retired' police officer, formally a senior instructor at the South Yorkshire Police dog training establishment.

I have 35 years experience in the training of dogs both within the police service and in the public sector.

I specialise in the development and training of specialist search dogs to include narcotics, explosives, currency, human remains, blood and semen.

OPERATION TASK CANINE DEPLOYMENTS 1-8 AUGUST 2007

On the instruction of The PJ Director, The Portuguese police kept all search records concerning the deployment of the search dogs. All dog searches were recorded by video.

The following searches were conducted:

Five apartments at a complex in Praia Da Luz.
Mr. Murat's property at Pria Da Luz.
Mr. McCann's Villa at Pria Da Luz (Present occupancy).
Articles of clothing from Mr. McCann's residence.
Western beach Pria da Luz.
Eastern Beach Pria Da Luz.
10 Vehicles screened at Portimao.

WESTERN BEACH

The beach above the waterline was searched. This extended to areas of fallen rock and the cliff face as far as the dog could negotiate the incline. **There were no alert indications.**

EASTERN BEACH

The beach above the waterline was searched. This extended to areas of fallen rock and the cliff face as far as the dog could negotiate the incline. **There were no alert indications.**

150.   How many 3 and 4 hour long lunch breaks did you take during the 4 months you were meant to be looking for Madeleine McCann?
151.   Do you always drink alcohol while on duty?

Exclusive: Disgrace of Madeline cop

http://www.mirror.co.uk/sunday-mirror/2007/09/30/exclusive-disgrace-of-madeleine-cop-98487-19870746/

Grant Hodgson In Praia Da Luz, sundaymirror.co.uk 30/09/2007

THE SEARCH FOR MADELEINE: DAY 150

Puffing on a cigarette and knocking back beers, the man leading the world's biggest missing child inquiry enjoys yet another long, boozy lunch.

Portuguese police chief Goncalo Amaral worked as little as four-and-a--half hours a day this week - despite a mountain of uninvestigated sightings of Madeleine McCann on his desk. And since the return from Portugal of Kate and Gerry McCann and most of the media covering the case, many in his squad have had their feet up, their main role seemingly to provide drinking companions for their boss.

His longest session, which lasted three hours and 10 minutes, was on Friday afternoon. It meant he could not have carried out more than four-and-a-half hours of work all day. Amaral, 47, who has a young daughter, is No3 in the Madeleine inquiry, in charge of its day-to-day running. After one drinking spree this week, the moustachioed police chief got in his car and drove home.

DIARY OF POLICE CHIEF AMARAL
1.15pm GO FOR LUNCH - 4.23pm BACK TO WORK

Wednesday: While the world hopes a young blonde girl seen in Morocco might be Madeleine, Amaral and his team have other priorities.

9.30am: Amaral arrives for work in his car wearing a beige jacket, jeans and a white shirt.

1.17pm: He casually strolls out of the police building and takes a leisurely stroll to the Carvi restaurant with his boss Guilhermino Encarnacao - dubbed Inspector Clueless - who is making a rare visit to the investigation.

Lunch: They share a bottle of wine white and two fish platters before heading back to the office at 3.27pm.

6.30pm: Amaral heads home.

Thursday: Amaral's boss has left town, meaning he can focus properly his lunch.

9.30am: He clocks on.

1.07pm: It's down tools time as he heads for lunch with a younger colleague.

1.15pm: They are joined by a Nancy Dell'Olio lookalike, who wears a figure-hugging black dress. The woman greets Amaral by patting him on the backside and ruffling his thinning hair.

1.20pm: The group move to Amaral's preferred secluded table. His first drink is a pinkcoloured fruit cordial but he's soon switching to a glass of Portuguese Sagres lager.

2.19pm: Amaral has a coughing fit which lasts more than three minutes. He splutters at the table, sipping water before picking up the bill for the £84 meal.

3.30pm: The woman leaves by herself and the men follow a few minutes' later.

6.13pm: Amaral emerges from the building with the colleague he went to lunch with. They return to the Carvi and sit watching the evening news on the TV.

6.48pm: The young man leaves after another beer. Amaral stays on, eating a couple of fish dishes.

9.55pm: After a few more beers, he heads back to his car and drives home.

Friday: 9.54am: Amaral pitches up for work even later than normal.

1.08pm: After fewer than three hours at his desk, he's off to pick up his daughter from school and brings her back to the Carvi with him.

1.15pm: He orders the first of at least four beers. He and his colleague also order a bottle of white wine while the little girl has a soft drink.

2.14pm: He takes his daughter back to the car. She is driven off and he is joined by two more friends and his racing driver friend. Amaral then has at least three more beers and a glass of wine.

4.23pm: It's nearly time to go home and, after splitting the bill and saying goodbye to his friend, Amaral and two of his colleagues slowly walk back to their office.

5.55pm: After just an hour and 32 minutes back at his desk, Amaral emerges into the bright afternoon sunlight carrying a white plastic bag and blue folder. He walks the short distance from his office to the underground car park.

6.10pm: After getting into his navy blue Volvo he heads for home, and the 148th day of the Madeleine hunt ends as it began - **in a hive of inactivity.**

---

152. Is it a part of your investigative techniques to talk about and reveal highly sensitive information during an ongoing high profile police investigation?

http://www.mirror.co.uk/sunday-mirror/2007/09/30/ex-clusive-disgrace-of-madeleine-cop-98487-19870746/

In a conversation with a Portuguese racing driver, he was heard saying he was sure the little girl was dead even though there's no final proof that she is. He told ex-F1 star Pedro Lamy he believed the McCanns drugged Madeleine to keep her quiet and accidentally killed her.

Amaral said: "The police case is we are sure the parents kiled Madeleine. They are both doctors and know about drugs. We are confident in our case." One of the group outrageously chipped in how he believed the couple could have taken cocaine on the night Madeleine disappeared.

The conversation was a flagrant breach of the judicial secrecy rules which prevent Kate and Gerry from defending themselves against police leaks. Amaral, his beer belly spilling over his baggy jeans and a creased shirt unbuttoned to reveal a gold medallion, looked more like a holidaymaker than a detective in charge of a case which today enters its 150th day.

---

153. It has been rumoured that there are a network of tunnels in Praia da Luz, that link the church, police station and beach amongst other places, if these tunnels exisit in any way shape or form, have they ever been searched?

154. This is important so to be clear we ask again - the files say that you took two photofit descriptions from two unconnected individual witnesses, these photofit descriptions were extremely alike and they both reported seeing a white van. What did you do about this? What investigations did you make and where is the official documentation that backs up what action you took?

---

155. May 5 - Portuguese police reveal they believe Madeleine was abducted but is still alive and in Portugal, and say they have a sketch of a suspect.

May 25 - Detectives finally release a description of the man reported by Jane Tanner three weeks earlier following pressure from the McCann's, their legal team and the British Government.

Why did it take the P J 20 days, and more importantly, so much pressure, to release a sketch of a suspect?

---

156. Why did you not release the e-fits of the possible abductor/abductors of two potentially vital witnesses?

http://www.thesun.co.uk/sol/homepage/news/maddie/article1520090.ece

Why did cops hide 2 e-fits?

From VERONICA LORRAINE
in Praia da Luz
Published: 06 Aug 2008

HIGHLY-detailed e-fits of two Maddie suspects were held back by Portuguese police, the official case files have revealed.

The images were created after two British witnesses reported seeing suspicious men hanging around Praia da Luz before Maddie disappeared. But, bizarrely, the public were never allowed to see them.

Instead, it was left to the McCanns to release a sketch of a suspect on October 25 – more than five months after Maddie disappeared on May 3.

It was drawn by an FBI-trained artist and based on the eyewitness account of Gerry and Kate's pal, Jane Tanner, 37. She believed she had seen a man taking Maddie.

But the figure in the sketch was faceless which made it virtually useless – while the "secret" police e-fits are so detailed they look more like photos.

The first was created after Brit Derek Flack – who has a holiday home in Praia da Luz – went to police on May 6.

The second e-fit was made from evidence given by local property developer Lance Purser, 45, a Brit originally from London.

He was shown another e-fit by cops of a potential suspect and told them he had seen someone similar about two weeks before Maddie disappeared. The suspect was aged 35 to 40 and wore jeans and a dark jacket. He had straight, dark collar-length hair. Mr Purser told cops that his face was "rustic looking" with sun-weathered skin and dark eyes.

The pal said: "It's outrageous that information relating to potential suspects seen in the area looking at the apartment so soon before the disappearance of Madeleine was not made available as a matter of extreme urgency.

"The early stages of this were crucial. Seeing these images has come as a shock to all concerned.

---

157. Is it true that other witnesses saw a man hanging around observing apartment 5a and he was using a white van?
158. Have you checked the possibility that this van may have belonged to one of the known paedophiles that were known to have been in Praia da Luz at the time that Madeleine McCann disappeared?

The first was created after Brit Derek Flack – who has a holiday home in Praia da Luz – went to police on May 6.

The 64-year-old had spotted a man staring "fixedly" at the McCanns' apartment and Mr Flack became convinced he was not a tourist. The police files describe how the man was so preoccupied by what he was doing he did not even notice he was being watched.

Mr Flack, president of his local Neighbourhood Watch group back in Ilford, Essex, told cops that he had seen the man either on the day Maddie disappeared or the day before. He described the suspect as tanned, of medium height and aged between 25 and 35.

The man had thick, dark hair and was wearing a light T-shirt, possibly yellow.

Mr Flack said he had initially associated the man *with a white Opel van,* parked nearby, because he was staring towards it.

The files show the van was only a short distance from a footpath at the back of the McCanns' Ocean Club block, which has access to their apartment's veranda.

Mr Flack believes the man was monitoring the movements near that path and into the apartment.

---

159. Is it true that, in your entire time as head of the investigation, you never once interviewed or spoke to the McCann's yourself?

The McCanns' spokesman, Clarence Mitchell, was seen in a TV interview to publicly slate the book 'The Truth of the Lie.' He further stated that Kate and Gerry are already planning to sue Goncalo Amaral, 48, over allegations in his book.

In this interview he said: "This account has gross inaccuracies and is grossly defamatory. "The conclusions are entirely false. They suggest Kate and Gerry were involved in the death, accidental or otherwise, of Madeleine and covered it up."

He added: "Mr Amaral and his publishers should not mistake a lack of action yet for any lack of long-term action. "He is presented as a world-class Madeleine expert but what does he know?

"Do you know how many times he interviewed Kate and Gerry when he was on the case - not once!"

---

160. Is it true you spent most of your career in the drug enforcement branch of the PJ, hunting down and prosecuting drug smugglers and suppliers?
161. If so, in what way do you think your past experience qualifies you to head the search for a missing little girl?
162. During this time, did you come into contact with any other smugglers of a different kind, e.g. child traffickers?

163. How humane did you think it was to leave two pan-icked and distraught parents who could not speak the language alone in a foreign country, while the Golden Abduction hours ticked by?

164. If this was your child and she was taken, is this the kind of investigation she would have received – answer truthfully?

165. If this was not your case, how would you look upon the person conducting it? (Answer TRUTHFULLY!)

166. Do you now accept that you have been comprehensively wrong about these parents?

167. How would you be able to face Madeleine and what would you say to her if/when she is found?

168. Do you have anything to say to the abductors?

9. HERE IS A SUMMARY OF ALL THE QUESTIONS WE DEMAND ANSWERS TOO, IN A MORE EASILY READ AND CLEAR FORMAT. WE ARE SURE YOU, TOO, CAN THINK OF MANY MORE.

1. You had a call from an English couple in deep distress, their daughter had vanished, the whole of PDL (except for Robert Murat) was out searching for her. Have you confirmed Robert Murat was not involved in the search??
2. How long after you knew that Madeleine had disappeared did you decide this was a case of a child wandering off and then instruct your men to go home and return the next morning if needed?
3. Do you always assume that small children going missing from their beds in the evenings have gone wandering off on their own in the dark?
4. How long did you sleep knowing that a small child was missing from her bed?

5. What time did the first call come in to which the GNR responded?
6. What time did the GNR request the PJ to come to the apartment?
7. Did you immediately dispatch teams of your men and the GNR to do preliminary searches?
8. Is it true that you never attended the scene yourself on the night Madeleine was abducted, but coordinated the investigation by phone? Where exactly did you coordinate this investigation from?
9. How was it possible to coordinate the search for a missing toddler over the telephone?
10. Did it not occur to you that there was a serious situation here and perhaps you had better get to the scene, take control and coordinate it properly?
11. On the night of May 3, 2007 how much had you had to drink after 18:00 hours?
12. If you had chosen to drive to Praia da Luz when the call for help was made on May 3, 2007 would you have been breaking the law?
13. Is that in fact one of the reasons you chose to coordinate from home?
14. Why did you expect distraught parents to do YOUR job and secure a crime scene?
15. In view that it was YOUR obligation and YOUR job to see that a crime scene is properly secured, why did YOU allow so many people to contaminate it?
16. Why did no one order the flat to be cleared of all people that should not be there and then order that it be cordoned off IMMEDIATELY?
17. Why did you not consider getting the apartment properly examined by properly trained forensics teams IMMEDIATELY?
18. Why did you leave this couple to do their own searching, while you stayed home in bed?

19. If you were home knowing that the crime scene was being contaminated, why then ask the parents why they allowed people into the apartment?
20. Why did you initially refuse Scotland Yard experts help?
21. Were you not worried about the preservation of the crime scene and being on the spot to put in place the routine for when a child goes missing? Were you not worried about missing the 'Golden Hours?'
22. If you never attended the scene that night, how do you know that Kate sat on Madeleine's bed traumatised unable to move?
23. If you did not attend the crime scene and view the bed for yourself, how could you say that the bed did not look like it had been slept in? In any event the bed did look like it had been slept in by a small child and it looked like someone had turned the bedclothes back to lift her out. Why did you say that the bed was hardly touched then accuse Kate of sitting on it?
24. To an ordinary person, you are told a child has gone missing; the first thing you do is to search the place. Behind the sofa, in the wardrobe, behind the curtains. Why do you think this is odd? Why did YOU not stop them?
25. Why did you not organise a search for the child IMMEDIATELY?
26. Why did you not order an immediate fingertip search at first light outside from where Madeleine went missing, instructing people what to look for, cigarette butts, matches, etc and tell them how to gather and secure this evidence?
27. Why did the police not carry out door to door searches immediately Madeleine was reported missing believed abducted?

28. Why did you not set an operations centre up in Mark Warner and order the lock down of the complex?
29. Why did you not ask MW manager for a list of all staff and all people holidaying that night?
30. Why did you not order the organisation of the immediate interviewing of all MW staff and residents?
31. Did you have a proper scene of crime room out of which to operate?
32. Have you taken DNA samples from all residents, all holiday makers and all staff present at MW on and shortly before May 3rd?
33. Why did you not order the Spanish borders with Portugal to be informed you had a missing child believed abducted and issue them with photographs and details?
34. Same with the Marina just short distance away, why did you not order the lock down of this Marina?
35. Why did you not inform authorities at the airport?
36. Why did it take you 24 hours after Madeleine went missing to alert all border controls?
37. Why did you allow Mark Warner cleaning staff to come in and clean apartment 5a and then ask Kate McCann why the flat had been cleaned
38. Why did you allow MW staff to enter this flat, a crime scene, and remove vital evidence such as the child's bedding?
39. Is it a possibility that the evidence of cleaning you have asked Mrs McCann about could have been the evidence of cleaning left by the MW cleaners that you allowed to enter and clean a crime scene in the first few days after Madeleine disappeared?
40. Is it possible that the apartment was then cleaned again by those allowed to rent the apartment weeks after Madeleine went missing?

41. Did you at anytime think that the abductor could have been putting up a pretence and was helping in searching the flat?
42. When the police finally did start searching, in what locations was Maddie searched for, how and in what manner?
43. Where were you during these searches, and what were you doing?
44. Why did you not organise an immediate 15K ring search centring on the area that Madeleine disappeared from?
45. How many flats have been searched in the MW complex and when were they searched?
46. When were the MW buildings searched? i.e. cellars, offices, backs of restaurants, empty apartments etc?
47. Did you organise an immediate search of all barns, gardens and cellars in the immediate vicinity?
48. Is it true that finger prints were not lifted from this apartment until five days after Madeleine went missing?
49. Is it true that the first finger prints lifted from the apartment were not taken properly and had to be re taken?
50. Why didn't the forensics technician taking the finger prints from the shutter and the bedroom window dress appropriately in accordance with international guidelines for taking forensic evidence?
51. Why do you think it strange that Kate's fingerprints were on the window, but not the abductors? Are you not aware that most criminals, with intent to break and enter, wear gloves?
52. Considering how important the shutter was to this investigation, why was the shutter not taken away and stripped down for proper analysis?

53. Is it true that proper forensic examination of this flat did not take place until Day 100 after Madeleine went missing?
54. When the McCann's moved out of this apartment, who else had access to it?
55. Was the flat cordoned off and kept locked and secured and was it guarded at all times by a police guard after the McCann's had moved out?
56. In your opinion could anyone have had sufficient time, motive and opportunity to plant evidence in that apartment?
57. Why did you allow apartment 5a to be used by numerous other holiday makers for two out of the three months since Madeleine disappeared?
58. Why were the bins in Luz allowed to be emptied shortly after Madeleine went missing?
59. Has the waste tip where the rubbish from Praia da Luz is taken been searched thoroughly for any signs of Madeleine, or her pyjamas or anything else missing?
60. When did you order a list of all paedophiles known to be in the area at this time?
61. Did you get in touch with the German police and the Swiss police about two paedophiles known to be in Praia da Luz at the time of Madeleine McCann's disappearance?
62. Did you yourself question all known witnesses that night of May 3rd?
63. Did you ask your men to ask for all witnesses to come forward and make a list of them before they left the apartment that night to go home to bed?
64. Is it true that the witness Mrs Pamela Fenn said she heard *A* child crying and did NOT say she heard *Madeleine* crying?

65. Did you think of asking the parents to ask the twins if they saw something? (Even though they were very small and asleep and you probably would not get a coherent logical answer?)
66. Mr McCann pointed out to you he thought it was odd that the twins remained asleep during all the commotion, did you not think of getting the twins tested and physically examined by a doctor immediately as he suggested?
67. Did you not think to come and help this couple who were alone in a foreign country unable to speak the language, alone panicking and petrified?
68. Why do you consider it strange that a member of the family contacted Sky News the following morning?
69. Why did you inform the press that the parents contacted Sky News BEFORE calling the police?
70. Did you consider cultural differences? Did you try to understand that publicity and advertising that a child has disappeared, using the media is how things are handled in Britain??
71. Why did you not order an immediate circulation of this child's picture, so people knew who they were looking for?
72. Why did you not issue a public appeal?
73. Do you as a serving detective, not know the European drill for a missing child believed abducted? Where circulating a photo to the media is considered of **VITAL** importance?
74. Were you aware of the 'Child Rescue Alert System' which has been employed across Europe since 2007? Which was actually in force at the time Madeleine McCann went missing?
75. If you did know of this drill, why did you not put the Bullet Point list into operation immediately?

76. Did you check the CCTV cameras of people coming in and leaving the resort?
77. Concerning you professional career, how many missing child/abduction cases have you investigated?
78. What was the outcome of those cases?
79. Is there any controversy over those cases?
80. Why did you think of bringing in sniffer dogs from the UK several months AFTER Madeleine went missing?
81. Are you aware of the FACT that two of the by-products of decomposition, putrescine and cadaverine, have been bottled and are commercially available as dog training aids?
82. Can this scent of death be produced in a laboratory for dog training purposes? Is this produced in any lab in Portugal? Have you checked to see if anyone had recently purchased such a product? Have you checked out all those that have access to such product?
83. Are you aware that these by-products are present in ALL decaying organic material, and also in human saliva?
84. Did you ever think that there may have been evidence left by the abductor/s that could have made the dogs react in this way?
85. Is it a possibility that such evidence could have been missed because you did not order the immediate securing of a crime scene?
86. Is it true that the blood found in the apartment 5a was found to be that of an Eastern European Male?
87. Is it possible that the blood indicated by the above was what the dogs reacted to?
88. Is it possible that the scent the dogs reacted to could have been placed there by previous holidaying occupants of apartment 5a before the McCann's arrived?

89. If you felt so strongly that the parents were involved then why allow them to drive their car in for examination?

90. When the cars were lined up to be exposed to the sniffer dogs, why did you allow this procedure to take place in a public car park and not a scientifically controlled scene?

91. When these cars were lined up to be exposed to the dogs, why did you allow the McCann's hire car to remain highly identifiable by allowing the find Madeleine bright yellow stickers all over it?

92. Is it true that the sniffer dogs walked past ALL cars in the line up, INCLUDING the McCann's hire car, indicating a NEGATIVE?

93. When the dogs walked past this vehicle and FAILED to indicate a positive reaction, why did you insist that they be brought back and walked around the car until they did indicate a positive?

94. Did you have any idea that the dogs may indicate a positive if they were repeatedly subjected to walking around this particular vehicle?

95. Bearing in mind the case of the Jersey Orphanage, where the dogs alerted to what later turned out to be a piece of coconut shell, how do you account for saying these dogs have never given a false sign in 200 cases?

96. Are you aware that in a similar case in the United States, a judge ruled out the evidence of sniffer dogs, saying they were 'no more reliable than the flip of a coin?'

97. Are you aware that one of the T-shirts the dog alerted to, was NOT Madeleine's, as you claimed, but in fact Shaun's?

98. Is it true that your OWN officers have expressed doubts about the dogs handling, and the way they reacted to the McCann's hire car?
99. If, as you recently claimed, Gerry buried Madeleine on the beach, why did the sniffer dogs not react to any of HIS clothes?
100. Did you even think of asking to have the dogs sniff his clothes?
101. Did you or any of your men have contact with dead or drowned human bodies prior to the sniffer dogs being brought to Portugal?
102. Is it true that ALL DNA evidence that has been found both inside the flat and the hire car is mitochondrial DNA which could have belonged to Madeleine, Amelie or Kate herself?
103. Is it true that you misinterpreted the DNA evidence from the FSS in Birmingham UK AND that from the Portuguese forensic science lab?
104. Why did you ignore the email from John Lowe of the FSS in Birmingham, three days BEFORE you made the McCanns arguidos, warning that the DNA samples were inconclusive? Why did you still proceeded to make The McCanns arguidos?
105. Why did you then LIE to Gerry about the DNA in the hire car? As previously stated, the British FSS made it clear that the test results were inconclusive, and should in no way form part of any investigation. Yet four days later, you lied to Gerry McCann, telling him the results were 100% positive. Is it usual to 'overstate the strength' of evidence in this way?
106. Have you traced, spoken to and checked out the professions and the occupants of those that rented the apartment after Madeleine went missing?

107. Is it true that pieces of paper which could have contained vital information in this investigation were just strewn about the PJ offices?
108. Is it true that the leaked report to the press of a boot print found inside the flat and on the bumper of the McCann's hire care was that of policeman belonging to the GNR?
109. Is it normal in Portugal for someone you suspect in the case you are investigating, (Robert Murat) to be allowed to translate during key witness interviews?
110. Why did you make them arguidos and then complain Kate would not answer questions, exercising her right to remain silent under the arguido status that you yourself placed her under?
111. If you wanted Kate to answer your questions, why didn't you leave her a witness, explaining that under Portuguese law, witnesses are obliged by law to answer police questions?
112. Did Kate refuse to answer the questions after the alleged deal -2 year jail sentence?
113. Did she stop answering questions on the advice of her Portuguese lawyer?
114. And how given the secrecy order, did the fact that she had not answered these questions leak out from the investigation you were then heading?
115. Is it true that you asked for the secrecy order to be implemented in this case?
116. Is it true that the secrecy law need NOT have been evoked in this case?
117. Did you make Mr and Mrs McCann aware of the FACT that the secrecy law need not be applied in the investigation and search for their missing daughter?
118. Is it true you made the McCann's arguidos "too hastily" just 8 days BEFORE the law was Due to change in Portugal?

119. Is it true that if you had waited to make the McCa-nn's arguidos, you would have had to produce hard and fast evidence to do so? Is it true that you made the McCann's arguidos then because you had NO evidence to back your suspicions?

120. Who do you think as been leaking highly sensitive reports to the Portuguese press?

121. Why do you think they would leak these confidential reports to the press?

122. From where did Felicia Cabrita obtain all her information and is it true that her husband is your lawyer "Antonio Cabrita"?

123. Have you ever had lunch with Felicia Cabrita?

124. How in your opinion did Felicia Cabrita get hold of this 'extreme' information? Where did she get copies of witness testaments, witness names, addresses and telephone numbers?

125. Is it true that you presided over a highly sensitive investigation where leaks from within this investigation were repeatedly used to blacken the characters of Kate and Gerry McCann?

126. Have you ever had any contact whatsoever, with Journalist Nacho Abad of Spanish television programme Ana Rosa Quintana?

127. Is it true that you dismissed many sightings, one in particular in Morocco, on the grounds that you assume Madeleine is dead and her parents are to blame?

128. Is it also true that a member of the hotel staff saw a man hiding in the bush near the McCanns apartment? And were there any footprints in the ground under that bush? If there were what was done about them? Were they investigated or ignored as many other sightings and leads appeared to have been? And if this is true, why?

129. Why was the car park outside Madeleine's window not checked for tyre prints?

130. Do you or anyone else that you know of have any financial assets which might suffer as a result of it becoming known that a child was abducted in the Algarve?

131. Did you hold any of those same conflicting interests when Joanna was abducted? (It is just a question not a statement)

132. In your opinion would a family oriented resort catering largely to British visitors suffer if it became known that a British child had been abducted by a human trafficking ring operating in the Algarve?

133. What date did your dog die and what contact did you have with the dog's cadaver?

134. According to rumours leaked about the McCanns from these sources "close to the PJ" the group were said to have drunk 14 bottles of wine on the night of May 3? The bill from the restaurant in your files indicates ONLY 2 bottle of wine and several bottles of non-alcoholic beverages (for the entire group) -- how would you explain that discrepancy?

135. And why was it leaked that they had drank more wine than you actually knew to be the case? If you were having dinner with a group of 9 people, would you have more than two bottles of wine on the table?

136. Why did it take you over a week to instruct police to visit the only supermarket near the Ocean Club?

137. Due to the very close proximity (about 7 miles) that Joanna Cipriano went missing did you ever consider that there may be a connection between the disappearances of Joanna and Madeleine?

138. How would you have handled a connection between these two missing children if it had emerged?

139. How often did you keep Mr & Mrs McCann updated on the progress of the search for their daughter?

140. Why did you tell the McCann's not to speak to the Spanish journalist who claimed he knew of a French paedophile who was on his way to Portugal for his next victim? Especially as you were informed that there was paedophile activity in the area?

141. Did you ever return alone to inspect apartment 5a during the 3 months after Madeleine disappeared?

142. Regarding the other arguido 'Robert Murat'. Police say they completely searched the villa, but detectives spent less than a full day collecting material and then allowed the family to return, leading some to question how thorough they actually were. It takes days to complete a thorough forensic search, so how thorough was this search and did it follow international guidelines for correct forensic procedure?

143. Who was this mysterious witness you were on the brink of producing, just prior to being removed from the case?

144. Why was this witness' details not passed on to the new head of the investigation, if his testimony you considered to be most important?

145. Is it true that there was no communication whatsoever between yourself and the new head of case? Is this normal behaviour, and can you explain this?

146. Why are you so adamant that Madeleine died in the apartment, yet are totally unable to explain why, with not one shred of evidence to back this 'hunch' up?

147. You recently claimed to believe that Gerry buried her on the beach. Why then, when Martin Grimes took the sniffer dogs to the beach, did they fail to react?

148. Are you aware that there are packs of stray dogs roaming the area? Is it not most likely that these dogs would have smelt a dead body and dug it up from the

beach, assuming holiday makers digging sandcastles had already not done so?

149. How likely is it that Gerry could have returned twenty six days later, disinterred the body, and moved it to a new burial place, under the full glare of the world's media, without being spotted?

150. How many 3 and 4 hour long lunch breaks did you take during the 4 months you were meant to be looking for Madeleine McCann?

151. Do you always drink alcohol while on duty?

152. Is it a part of your investigative techniques to talk about and reveal highly sensitive information during an ongoing high profile police investigation?

153. It has been rumoured that there are a network of tunnels in Praia da Luz, that link the church, police station and beach amongst other places, if these tunnels exisit in any way shape or form, have they ever been searched?

154. This is important so to be clear we ask again - the files say that you took two photofit descriptions from two unconnected individual witnesses, these photofit descriptions were extremely alike and they both reported seeing a white van. What did you do about this? What investigations did you make and where is the official documentation that backs up what action you took?

155. May 5 - Portuguese police reveal they believe Madeleine was abducted but is still alive and in Portugal, and say they have a sketch of a suspect.

May 25 - Detectives finally release a description of the man reported by Jane Tanner three weeks earlier following pressure from the McCann's, their legal team and the British Government.

Why did it take the P J 20 days, and more importantly, so much pressure, to release a sketch of a suspect?

156. Why did you not release the e-fits of the possible abductor/abductors of two potentially vital witnesses?

157. Is it true that other witnesses saw a man hanging around observing apartment 5a and he was using a white van?

158. Have you checked the possibility that this van may have belonged to one of the known paedophiles that were known to have been in Praia da Luz at the time that Madeleine McCann disappeared?

159. Is it true that, in your entire time as head of the investigation, you never once interviewed or spoke to the McCann's yourself?

160. Is it true you spent most of your career in the drug enforcement branch of the PJ, hunting down and prosecuting drug smugglers and suppliers?

161. If so, in what way do you think your past experience qualifies you to head the search for a missing little girl?

162. During this time, did you come into contact with any other smugglers of a different kind, e.g. child traffickers?

163. How humane did you think it was to leave two panicked and distraught parents who could not speak the language alone in a foreign country, while the Golden Abduction hours ticked by?

164. If this was your child and she was taken, is this the kind of investigation she would have received – answer truthfully?

165. If this was not your case, how would you look upon the person conducting it? (Answer TRUTHFULLY!)

166. Do you now accept that you have been comprehensively wrong about these parents?

167. How would you be able to face Madeleine and what would you say to her if/when she is found?

168. Do you have anything to say to the abductors?

10. The Key Blunders.

According to the Portuguese official case files, it took the Policia Judiciaria (PJ) virtually two months to seal off the apartment where Madeleine McCann disappeared from and treat it as a major crime scene. This monumental blunder meant that vital information that could have helped track the toddler, was lost to the investigation for ever.

Apartment 5a should have been subject to a thorough forensic investigation, but it was not sealed off properly and members of the public could get very close to the scene, thus further destroying any clues which may have been left by any abductors in the roads surrounding the apartment. To the best of our knowledge, an essential properly organised forensic finger tip search/examination of the roads, walks and car park surrounding the apartment was never carried out. This was despite reports from eye witnesses saying that they had noted suspicious activity outside.

TV footage captured a Portuguese forensic technician dusting the shutters for finger prints, the technician's hair was loose and blowing in the wind, she only wore one glove. This is against international standards for gathering forensic material, cross contamination could have occurred and one thumb print found on the shutters, was found to belong to an investigating officer and did not belong to Kate McCann, as was widely reported at the time. Considering the vital importance of these shutters to the abduction, as they were found open by Kate when she discovered Madeleine missing, this was yet another monumental error on behalf of the investigating officers.

Apartment 5a lay empty for a month after Madeleine vanished, but amazingly it was then freed from the investigation and the owner allowed to let it to three different families of holiday makers, thus contaminating the crime scene further. A total number of NINE people were allowed to contaminate a serious and major crime scene.

No conclusive DNA samples were ever found.

The apartment was eventually sealed off in August, almost 3 months after Madeleine disappeared, this happened after UK trained sniffer dogs were brought in. Further DNA samples were then taken because the dogs alerted in the apartment and seemed to suggest evidence of Madeline's DNA, but nothing conclusive was ever discovered from those samples, which were tested by the Forensic Science Services in Birmingham.

In fact it would have been more of a surprise if Madeleine's DNA wasn't found in that apartment.

Further, it is unclear if DNA samples were ever taken from the 9 different people allowed to stay in the flat before it was eventually made a crime scene, so it is unclear if any other DNA discovered in that apartment, was ever ruled out or ruled in, or investigated, as coming from a possible abductor. After each family stayed in the apartment, it was then cleaned by Mark Warner staff, further reducing to zero the chance of discovering any worthwhile DNA samples. Kate was blamed for cleaning the apartment, when in fact it was cleaning staff who carried this procedure out and they were given the OK to do this by detectives conducting the investigation.

The Portuguese press made much of blood being found in the apartment, but after forensic DNA tests, this turned out to be the blood from a holiday maker who had previously stayed in the apartment, who cut himself shaving. Witness testaments have been given to this extent by the people concerned, who themselves got in touch with the PJ to explain what had happened.

Full details of those who stayed in the apartment were given to Goncalo Amaral, who was then the lead detective, this was before Amaral was sacked form the investigation, for personally attacking the British police in the Portuguese press.

Bodily fluids were supposed to have been found in the car, but these were later confirmed as possible urine and faecal matter, which could have come from Madeleine's twin siblings used nappies, which were transported in the car boot when moving from the apartment to the villa, prior to being disposed of. The nappies were transported like this because they were to be thrown in garbage bins which are kept in the roads away from the apartments in Praia da Luz, there was no place to leave soiled nappies in the apartment.

In particular, video film of Eddie the cadaver scenting dog showed he had to be harshly commanded back to the McCann hire car at least 5 times BEFORE indicating a positive, until then he showed no real interest in indicating a positive find.

Eddie indicated at the seal of the car on the drivers door, he did NOT indicate at the boot of the car, which is where you would expect the scent to be at its strongest, if as Goncalo Amaral has claimed with unsubstantiated comments, a 25 day old corpse was transported in the boot of the car! The dog's handler, Martin Grimes, was heard to say on the video footage, that because the dog had indicated at the seal, he did not intend to put the dog inside the car. The blood scenting dog 'Keela' was put into the boot of the car, but tried to jump out a few times before she indicated a positive, which turned out to be a negative, in other words Keela indicated a false positive.

The actual time Eddie, the cadaver scenting dog, was allowed to spend at the control cars used in the experiment was approximately 2/3 seconds, however when it came to the McCanns hire car, the dog was forced to spend as much time as was needed before he indicated a positive. At one point the dog was seen paying more attention to another car and running off in all directions and running around in circles between the cars, paying no attention at all the McCann hire car. The hire car was only rented by the McCann's, 25 days AFTER Madeleine disappeared, if these dogs are as good as they say, it is hard to understand how the dog had so much trouble indicating a positive to the transportation of a 25 day old corpse! One would be safe to assume that it would be relatively easy for the dog to indicate a strong positive and it would also be safe to assume that there would be evidence of a 25 day old corpse all over the car and not just on a six inch square of boot carpet, which in fact later proved totally inconclusive.

However, it was reported it was largely on this sniffer dog 'supposed' evidence, that Goncalo Amaral made Mr Mrs McCann suspects in the disappearance of their daughter.

If Goncalo Amaral had left the doctors as witnesses, instead of making them arguido and arguida (suspects), then under Portuguese law they would have been legally required to answer any questions put to them by investigating officers, so it is a mystery as to why Goncalo Amaral complained because they used their right to remain silent under interrogation, a right afforded to them under Portuguese law and awarded to them by Amaral himself. It was under specific instruction from their Portuguese lawyers, that Kate McCann remained silent during questioning. Much was made of Kate remaining silent, but when the famous forty questions were published, it is hard to see one that could have been useful in finding Madeleine, in fact, such was the quality of the questions, it was hard to see what good they would be to the investigation, they seemed more designed to take the onus away from the blunders of the investigation, rather than serve any useful purpose in finding Madeleine, or what happened that evening of May 3rd.

During an eight hour interrogation, detectives went on to tell Mr McCann, that his daughter's DNA had been found in the boot of the vehicle which was rented more than three weeks after she vanished! The official files have disclosed that Portuguese detectives knew there was no conclusive evidence against the McCanns three days before they interviewed them and made them suspects!

A friend of the doctors has been quoted as saying;

*"Serious questions need to be asked about why this was put to Gerry **as fact**. It was sloppy at best and **deliberately manipulative** at worst.*

"A number of senior officers went down the route of making assumptions and suppositions and trying to force a confession to something that didn't happen."

Further Clarence Mitchell, the couple's media spokesman said;

"I can confirm that the Portuguese police put it to Gerry as a fact that Madeleine's DNA had been found in both the apartment and the vehicle when it is now clear that the initial FSS report had made no such claim

"You have to ask yourself what the police were trying to achieve by overstating evidence that they didn't have, nor could claim to have.

"One wonders, under those circumstances, what the motivation was."

"The Portuguese Attorney General made it very clear indeed that there's absolutely no evidence of any wrongdoing by Kate and Gerry in any way, shape or form."

"A lot of this is historical detail drafted by officers who failed to find Madeleine and who quite wrongfully were going down inaccurate lines of supposition and assumption."

An email written by John Lowe of the FSS four days earlier on September 3 stated that the analysis of the samples in the car had proved nothing.

The email, which was translated into Portuguese on 4th September, warned that the samples could match huge sections of the population, including himself.

Mr Lowe said; the result was *"too complex for meaningful interpretation or inclusion"*.

Bizarrely in another twist if Goncalo Amaral had waited just another 8 days, he would **not** have been able to make Mr Mrs McCann suspects, because of a law change in Portugal and evidence would have been required before Amaral would have been allowed to make suspects.

The Portuguese police never had any evidence so they simply would not have been allowed to make them suspects.

Carlos Pinto de Abreu, the doctors Portuguese lawyer said, that under Portugal's new penal code, police must have more than just suspicions to make somebody an arguido.

"On September 15 a new procedural penal code was introduced making it necessary for there to be evidence against the citizen before they could be made an arguido.

"Before this date it wasn't necessary. You could be made an arguido without actual evidence against you," quoted Mr Pinto de Abreu.

The many blunders that were made by the Portuguese police were revealed in the extensive 30,000 page police dossier into the investigation.

Criticism of Portuguese police for missing key forensic evidence, and failing to bring in outside expertise earlier in the investigation.

The apartment had been "released" as a crime scene by Portuguese police on 11th June 2008, it was then cleaned and rented out to three other families, a total of at least nine people stayed in this apartment, after it should have been sealed and turned into a major crime scene from day one and a thorough forensic examination conducted.

Questions need to be raised as to why this took 3 months to happen and answers 'must' be forthcoming. It is simply not good enough that the Portuguese police and judicial, appear to be trying to stick their heads in the sand, behaving like ostriches is not going to prevent these catastrophic errors from happening again.

The Portuguese police seem inept and totally incapable and inexperienced in handling an investigation of this magnitude. It rendered the whole investigation open to accusations of bungling, ineptitude, chaos and farce.

Startling blunders have been highlighted which helped lead this investigation into the ensuing chaos and farce, that has a little girl 'still missing' and apparently vanished off the face of the earth.

1). At first officers played down suggestions that Madeleine had been abducted and believed she had just wandered off. The crime scene in and around the hotel was not cordoned off obliterating any chance of obtaining vital forensic evidence, which may have lead to clues into discovering Madeleine's whereabouts. It is also unclear if the detective in charge of the investigation actually attended the scene on the night Madeleine vanished from apartment 5a. It has been reported that Goncalo Amaral has never even spoken to Mr Mrs McCann, during the whole four months he headed this investigation.

2). No proper coordinated specialist fingertip searching in the car park or the streets around the apartment, meant more opportunities to find vital forensic evidence were lost. It had been reported that there was suspicious activity outside apartment 5a, but any evidence from this was lost. One senior British detective who now works for the media dubbed the scene "the worst preserved" he had witnessed in his career.

3). No incident room was set up at Mark Warner complex and officers failed to make early house-to-house inquiries when potential witnesses were still likely to be in the resort. Abduction experts agree that the first couple of hours following an abduction are crucial to recovering the child and these 'Golden Hours' after Madeleine's abduction, so vital to her, were totally lost. Only more than 48 hours later, on the Saturday after Madeleine went missing, did the Portuguese Police start searching some local apartments. A full list of guests staying at Mark Warner was only obtained on Sunday after Madeleine disappeared and the staff at Mark Warner's complex were only questioned 60 hours after Madeleine disappeared.

4). At the time of going to print with this book, there are allegedly still people in the same apartment block as Mr and Mrs McCann who have never been questioned. While empty properties yards from where Madeleine was reported to have been abducted, have never been searched, again missing vital clues.

5). CCTV on the main road out of Praia da Luz, going towards Spain, was not checked by police.

6). Police failed to inform Spanish borders that there had been an abduction and no description of Madeleine, or details of Madeleine's disappearance was given to Spanish border authorities until the morning after she was taken. This gave any would be abductors plenty of time to flee Portugal. It has been said that Madeleine was abducted and taken by road to Tarifa in Spain, where they crossed on the Tangiers's ferry into North Africa. The abductors would have had plenty of time to do this completely unchallenged by unknowing Spanish authorities.

7). Early witness descriptions created confusion, with many different E-fit images being shown to local people, the most famous one being, a childlike drawing of an egg with hair! It later emerged in the official files, that there were two strikingly similar E-fit images given by two separate individual witnesses, of a man standing next to a white van, near the rear entrance outside apartment 5a.

8). On the morning of May 7 and against Portuguese police advice Gerry and Kate McCann were force to issue their own televised appeal direct to the abductor. Then six hours later at a rare Portuguese police press conference, this appeal was totally undermined, when a police chief apparently said "We are not 100 per cent certain she was abducted."

9). Detectives said they could not issue information about the investigation owing to Portuguese "judicial secrecy". However, it should be noted that Portuguese law includes two exceptions, both of which apply in the case of Madeleine. Police could have if they wanted not employed the rule of Portuguese "judicial secrecy" and this investigation could have been open and help requested from the public.

10). Due to the "judicial secrecy" laws being unnecessarily applied, it meant no direct appeal for help was made to the public and police actually failed to give a clear description of Madeleine. There were no posters put up in the early days of the investigation, it was left to Madeleine's traumatised parents to describe what she was wearing on the night she disappeared and try to garner public attention to help search for their daughter.

11). An appeal for a suspect was finally issued 22 days after Madeleine went missing, together with a description. However the PJ made yet another catastrophic blunder when they issued, two different height descriptions, apparently as the result of a mistranslation.

12). Helicopters were not used very much during the search for Madeleine and on 9th May, the search was scaled down and searches were not very visible.

13). There are many wells in rough land surrounding Praia da Luz, and these have NEVER been investigated, nor any searched and the British sniffer dogs trained to scent cadaver, were never taken to these areas to search.

14). Despite Britain offering help and assistance from our own highly experienced officers, help was at first refused and there was a delay in calling in specialists. Not until one full week later were two British child abduction experts flown in and mobile phone tracker technicians who helped in the Soham investigation came in very late into the case.

15). Leaks, smears and innuendo have hampered the inquiry. On May 16, Portuguese newspapers reported that police were "on the trail" of a Russian friend of Robert Murat, the formal suspect in the case. He was only detained for questioning after he had been traced by journalists. Later Robert Murat, Sergy Malinka and Michaela Murat's girlfriend, were awarded damages for libel in the British High Court against national newspapers.

16). Madeleine's favourite toy "Cuddle cat" could have been a crucial key in tracking her down. She took it to bed with her every night including the night she disappeared. The toy was left behind when Madeleine was taken and the abductor could have left some trace of DNA evidence on it, but the Portuguese police did not check it out and it was not until months later after Mrs McCann took the toy with her everywhere, that it was sent off for forensic examination. According to specialists it was said that scientists would have needed to examine it for at least several days. When it was finally sent off for forensic examination it was probably far too late. The specialist said "It's an absolute glaring error."

17). On one of the video footage taken by the Portuguese police when the apartment was being searched using the British sniffer dog 'Eddie', the dog was clearly seen in the lounge area, taking the toy out of a container that the dog had pulled over, throwing it up in the air and trotting off after ignoring it, paying it no further attention. Later on the same footage, the toy had been removed from the lounge area and placed inside a cupboard in a different room and Eddie was then seen to bark a positive reaction at the same toy, he had previously ignored in the other room.

No explanation was given as to how the toy travelled from the lounge and placed in the cupboard of a different room, or who placed it there and what this person had been doing prior to them touching the toy. Certainly no explanation was given as to why only after the toy had been moved into a different location, did the dog bark a positive indication at it.

18). Portuguese police wanted to bug Mr and Mrs McCann to eavesdrop on their conversation, during the search for Madeleine according to the police files.

Coming in the shape of two bugs one in the house and one in the couple's car but a Portuguese judge refused the formal request, saying that the couple's witness statement would be enough, and that there was no evidence on which to grant such a request.

19). Many sightings of Madeleine, went uninvestigated and were disregarded by the PJ as not important.

The British end of the investigation, was co-ordinated by DC John Hughes, from Leicestershire Police, and looked into a spate of reports of children resembling the missing girl seen in Malta. In an e-mail dated June 26 last year he wrote: "Most replies we get back from other countries don't take us far as many can't be verified or discounted, and I feel these will be the same." Officially the investigation was shelved on 21st July 2008 and Mr Mrs McCann were cleared of any wrongdoing and their suspect status was dropped after it was reported that all leads went cold.

Portuguese prosecutors announced o July 21ˢᵗ 2008 that there was insufficient evidence and that the case was officially closed, but said the case could be reopened if credible new evidence comes to light. Ex-police officer Gonçalo Amaral who was lead detective on the Madeleine investigation and who was sacked after four months and later retired from police service under a cloud, has published his own version of events in a book which maintained that Mr and Mrs McCann were involved in their daughter's disappearance. It should be made abundantly clear that this is his own version of what happened, and that he does NOT have a shred of evidence with which to back up his often bizarre and unsubstantiated claims. Goncalo Amaral was also in charge of the investigation when allegedly there were leaks emanating from the PJ, appearing in the Portuguese press, often fuelling distrust and hate campaigns, which were springing up across the internet, on hate forums and blogs and the harassing and hounding of Mr Mrs McCann on the internet, is still going on to this very day

11. KATE'S 48 QUESTIONS.

The official files revealed that Portuguese police told Gerry McCann, they had found incriminating DNA from his missing daughter Madeleine.

This was said to have taken place during the time Mr Mrs McCann were interrogated by Portuguese police prior to being made 'arguido' and 'arguida' (suspects) in the disappearance of their daughter Madeleine.

It was also recorded to have happened four days AFTER scientists from the 'Forensic Science Services' (FSS) in Birmingham, warned the Portuguese judicial police, that the DNA said to have been found in the apartment and the hire car, could have come from anyone.

The DNA said to have been harvested from the hire car, rented crucially, 25 days AFTER Madeleine disappeared, was said to have been called 'inconclusive' by scientists carrying out the tests. This means the DNA could have come from a large number of the population.

But, never-the-less, Kate and Gerry McCann were still made suspects on the back of totally inconclusive evidence and the Portuguese police actually told Gerry McCann that his daughter's DNA was found.

We will leave you to form your own conclusions as to why Mr Mrs McCann were lied to and then made suspects on the back of non existent evidence. But would point out here, as has been afore mentioned, the law in Portugal actually changed 8 days after Mr Mrs McCann were made suspects in September 2007. If the lead detective who was then 'Goncalo Amaral' had waited a further 8 days, he would have had to have provided actual evidence in order to make them suspects, evidence he did not have!

Perhaps it should be asked of Mr Amaral and the Portuguese prosecutor what the rush was to make Mr Mrs McCann suspects? After all at this point, it was over four months since Madeleine had vanished from apartment 5a at the Ocean Holiday complex. Four months of seemingly nothing much happening in the investigation. At the time it was widely known that the doctors had already decided to return to England and were only waiting for Mr Amaral to complete this part of the investigation, and for the Portuguese judiciary to grant them permission to return to England.

Permission was subsequently granted by the Portuguese prosecutor for Mr Mrs McCann to return to England and Mr Amaral a member of the Policia Judiciaria, did not raise any objections to this.

Mr Goncalo Amaral, was unceremoniously sacked from the Madeleine investigation after insulting the British police soon after he made Mr Mrs McCann suspects.

Mr Amaral has since taken early retirement and is currently standing trial in Portugal over the alleged torture of Leonor Cipriano, mother of another missing Portuguese child 'Joana Cipriano'. This is covered in depth in another chapter in this book.

Mr Amaral has also said to have made many thousands of euros out of writing his own account in a book about what happened to Madeleine, but has yet to provide any real evidence in which to back his sometimes bizarre claims up. Mr Amaral has also raked in many thousands of euros in the form of TV and radio interviews, selling his story to newspapers and magazines etc.

The 20,000 - page 'Madeleine File' detailing the 14 month Portuguese investigation was opened up to the public and in doing so, some astonishing blunders and tactics by the PJ were also revealed.

'The dossier includes lines of inquiry pursued by detectives, forensic reports, witness statements and transcripts of interviews with the McCanns.'

'One such file reveals that Kate McCann refused to answer 48 specific questions put to her during an 11 hour interview in which police ask her directly whether she had anything to do with her daughter's disappearance.'

However as mentioned above and in another chapter of this book, an email from British scientist John Lowe, part of the major incidents team at the Birmingham-based

Forensic Science Service (FSS) on September 3, 2007, 'that provides a damning indictment of the controversial Portuguese investigation.'

Mr Lowe stated that a sample take from the Renault hire car, hired 25 days AFTER Madeleine disappeared, showed just 15 out of the 19 components of Madeleine's DNA, said to be required for a positive match, in other words, this test carried out on 'low copy' DNA, was inconclusive and could have belonged to anybody, including the person carrying out the test! Mr Lowe warned, that this test was way too complex for any 'meaningful' interpretation to be placed on the results. ('Low Copy' DNA, uses minute samples of DNA.)

Scientist 'Mr Lowe wrote:' *Let's look at the question that is being asked: ' Is there DNA from Madeleine on the swab?*

'It would be very simple to say 'Yes' simply because of the number of components within the result that are also in her reference sample.

'What we need to consider, as scientists, is whether the match is genuine - because Madeleine has deposited DNA as a result of being in the car or whether Madeleine merely appears to match the result by chance.'

Mr Lowe then pointed out that components of the missing girl's DNA were not unique to her - in fact, some of them were present among FSS scientists, including himself.

He stressed that low copy analysis couldn't determine when or how the DNA was deposited, what body fluid it came from - and whether a crime had been committed.

He concluded : 'We cannot answer the question: is the match genuine, or is it a chance match.'

Yet on this, Gerry McCann was told that there was 'evidence' that Madeleine's DNA had been found and the McCanns, were then made suspects!

Details of the 8 hour interrogation of Mr McCann, were among documents released in the official police files, which showed Mr McCann's interview was **not** recorded but an unidentified police officer's notes of the questioning were included in the files!

Apparently when Mr McCann was told that Madeleine's DNA had been gathered from behind the sofa and the boot of the hire car he was told that, the sample had been analysed by a British laboratory, Gerry McCann said he could not explain why this would be.'

The McCanns are keen not to give 'a running commentary' on their legal team's trawl through the files and to their credit, this remains the case today. The parents just want to be allowed to get on and search for their daughter.

There's absolutely no evidence of any wrongdoing by Kate and Gerry in any way, shape or form in the police files.

A lot of this is historical detail drafted by officers who failed to find Madeleine and who quite wrongfully were going down inaccurate lines of supposition and assumption. This remains the case today, with various ex Policia Judiciaria writing books and holding a high profile in the media.

"Kate and Gerry McCann are no longer arguidos. The Portuguese judicial system has accepted that they were not involved in Madeleine's disappearance in any way, there is absolutely nothing to suggest that Madeleine is dead and while this is the case, Mr Mrs McCann and their team will continue the search for Madeleine."

On 21st July 2008 the Portuguese prosecutors announced they were officially shelving the case, although it can be reopened if credible new evidence comes to light.

The dossier also showed that when interrogated, Kate McCann refused to answer 48 questions when quizzed by Portuguese police over her missing daughter. Much has been made of this, but it has emerged that Kate McCann was acting under instruction from her Portuguese lawyer. Also it should be noted that Kate McCann was only acting within the law and rights given to her under Portuguese law.

Had Mr Amaral decided to make her and Gerry 'official witnesses' then they would have been duly required under Portuguese law to answer all questions put to them, however this was NOT the case.

"Mrs McCann, a former GP, was subjected to 11 hours of interrogations at Portimao police station on 7th September 2007, four months after Madeleine disappeared.

The case files showed she faced very odd questioning over her relationship with her oldest child."

THE 48 QUESTIONS.

1. On May 3 2007, around 22:00, when you entered the apartment, what did you see? What did you do? Where did you look? What did you touch?
2. Did you search inside the bedroom wardrobe? (She replied that she wouldn't answer)
3. (Shown 2 photographs of her bedroom wardrobe) can you describe its contents?
4. Why had the curtain behind the sofa in front of the side window (whose photo was shown to her) been tampered with? Did somebody go behind that sofa?
5. How long did your search of the apartment take after you detected your daughter Madeleine's disappearance?
6. Why did you say from the start that Madeleine had been abducted?
7. Assuming Madeleine had been abducted, why did you leave the twins home alone to go to the 'Tapas' and raise the alarm? Because the supposed abductor could still be in the apartment.
8. Why didn't you ask the twins, at that moment, what had happened to their sister or why didn't you ask them later on?
9. When you raised the alarm at the 'Tapas' what exactly did you say and what were your exact words?
10. What happened after you raised the alarm in the 'Tapas'?
11. Why did you go and warn your friends instead of shouting from the veranda?
12. Who contacted the authorities?
13. Who took place in the searches?
14. Did anyone outside of the group learn of Madeleine's disappearance in those following minutes?

15. Did any neighbour offer you help after the disappearance?
16. What does 'we let her down' mean?
17. Did Jane tell you that night that she'd seen a man with a child?
18. How were the authorities contacted and which police force was alerted?
19. During the searches, with the police already there, where did you search for Maddie, how and in what way?
20. Why did the twins not wake up during that search or when they were taken upstairs?
21. Who did you phone after the occurrence?
22. Did you call Sky News?
23. Did you know the danger of calling the media, because it could influence the abductor?
24. Did you ask for a priest?
25. By what means did you divulge Madeleine's features, by photographs or by any other means?
26. Is it true that during the searches you remained seated on Maddie's bed without moving?
27. What was your behaviour that night?
28. Did you manage to sleep?
29. Before travelling to Portugal did you make any comment about a foreboding or a bad feeling?
30. What was Madeleine's behaviour like?
31. Did Maddie suffer from any illness or take any medication?
32. What was Madeleine's relationship like with her brother and sister?
33. What was Madeleine's relationship like with her brother and sister, friends and school mates?
34. As for your professional life, in how many and which hospitals have you worked?
35. What is your medical specialty?

36. Have you ever done shift work in any emergency services or other services?
37. Did you work every day?
38. At a certain point you stopped working, why?
39. Are the twins difficult to get to sleep? Are they restless and does that cause you uneasiness?
40. Is it true that sometimes you despaired with your children's behaviour and that left you feeling very uneasy?
41. Is it true that in England you even considered handing over Madeleine's custody to a relative?
42. In England, did you medicate your children? What type of medication?
43. In the case files you were SHOWN CANINE forensic testing films, where you can see them marking due to detection of the scent of human corpse and blood traces, also human, and only human, as well as all the comments of the technician in charge of them. After watching and after the marking of the scent of corpse in your bedroom beside the wardrobe and behind the sofa, pushed up against the sofa wall, did you say you couldn't explain any more than you already had?
44. When the sniffer dog also marked human blood behind the sofa, did you say you couldn't explain any more than you already had?
45. When the sniffer dog marked the scent of corpse coming from the vehicle you hired a month after the disappearance, did you say you couldn't explain any more than you already had?
46. When human blood was marked in the boot of the vehicle, did you say you couldn't explain any more than you already had?
47. When confronted with the results of Maddie's DNA, whose analysis was carried out in a British laboratory, collected from behind the sofa and the boot of the ve-

hicle, did you say you couldn't explain any more than you already had?

48. Did you have any responsibility or intervention in your daughter's disappearance?

Kate McCann did however, answer this question:

Q. Are you aware that in not answering the questions you are jeopardising the investigation, which seeks to discover what happened to your daughter?

A. 'Yes, if that's what the investigation thinks.'

By the time these questions were answered, it would have been clear both to Kate McCann and her legal representation, what lines the PJ were actually going along and to answer these questions, would heavily implicate Mrs McCann's position.

Mrs McCann has been accused of impeding the search for Madeleine by not answering these questions, but it is hard to see that four months on, how any of these questions could have lead to where the child was or was taken. Surely these are the kind of questions that should have been asked by Goncalo Amaral immediately? Remembering there is significant doubt as to Mr Amaral even attending the scene when Madeleine first went missing, in fact there are reports that Mr Amaral and his successor 'Mr Paulo Rebelo' have 'NEVER' actually spoken to Mr or Mrs McCann in person.

The often bizarre questions, look like they are a missmash taken from the various hate sites that have sprung up on the internet, concerning the investigation of Madeleine McCann.

12. SUMMARY.

There has been much made of the British sniffer dog evidence, not least by Goncalo Amaral himself, both before and after he got sacked from the Madeleine McCann investigation. But also by an ex solicitor by the name of Tony Bennett.

Tony Bennett has said much about the "so-called" sniffer dog evidence, both his wild claims and the claims of Goncalo Amaral, we believe, have been systematically discredited here. We have used the truth and not fanciful writings such as this excerpt take from Tony Bennett's website;

"There was a dead body in Apartment 5A. There was a dead body in the Renault Scenic hired by the McCanns. That dead body could only be one individual - already dead - who could have been in both Apartment 5A and in the Renault Scenic. It must have been Madeleine McCann." By Tony Bennett.

It is hard to imagine that anyone with a modicum of common sense could write such a thing, let alone an 'ex-solicitor', when there has been absolutely no evidence to back up such claims. Indeed the Portuguese chief prosecutor has said there is no evidence to say Madeleine is alive, and there is no evidence to say Madeleine is dead, yet still Bennett writes these fanciful claims and claims such as this also appear in his book of suggestions. Our aim is to state the truth, and wherever possible back that truth up with quotes. You will find a bibliography of websites at the end of this book, which may give some credence to the written works here.

You may remember 'Tony Bennett', was the solicitor who tried and failed to take a private prosecution against Michael Barrymore. Bennett has also tried and failed to bring a private prosecution for neglect, against Kate and Gerry McCann. Tony Bennett was also found guilty by the 'Law Society' for bringing his profession into disrepute.

When the police finally did start searching for Madeleine, the original Portuguese sniffer dogs used were reportedly not fit for the type of search they were used for. According to the Public Ministry archiving report, dated 21st July 2008. The report signed by prosecutors Magalhães e Menezes and João Melchior Gomes, states that this was likely to be a meaningless exercise as the Dogs used weren't trained for "urban areas". The animals had only been trained to follow scents in the countryside - Madeleine, who was almost 4 years old, when she vanished from her family's holiday apartment, in a small but busy TOWN. The dogs for this search, the Portuguese GNR dogs, were said to have tried to trace Madeleine through a blanket she had used. Unfortunately this was not adequate. Had the proper type of dogs been brought in at this point, they may have picked up a vital scent off of Madeleine. The trackers and their handlers weren't brought in for five days after Madeleine disappeared - even though experts said they should have been there within 48 hours. The really damning indictment is, when the dogs did finally arrive in Praia da Luz, they gave up the hunt after just 100 yards because they were confused by the stench of rotting food from a pile of bin-bags.

This means that all the clues that could have been found by adequately trained dogs and their handlers were missed. Correctly trained dogs were not taken to vacant apartments in the Mark Warner Ocean complex. They were not taken to cellars, or service areas of the Ocean Complex. Neither were they taken to garden sheds, basements, gardens, housing equipments for swimming pools barns, out houses, near to where Madeleine disappeared and the dogs were not taken to search the scrubland surrounding Praia da Luz.

There were also doubts raised from some involved in the investigation, about the accuracy of the British sniffer dogs Eddie and Keela.

(Eddie is trained to scent cadaverine and Keela is trained to scent blood.)

From Pages 1-3004 of the official report, Central Department of Criminal Investigation, February, 8th, 2008 The British dogs, 'Eddie the cadever dog' and 'Keela the blood scenting dog', were not brought in until 3 months after Madeleine disappeared!

When the videos of the dogs at work were screened, doubts arose about the technique and it was reported in the official reports that further clarification was required about certain points and actions by dog and handler in the videos.

The cadaver dog (Eddie) was seen passing the McCann hire car in an uninterested way. He finally signalled in the place (The hire car) only after he had past uninterested no less than FIVE TIMES before. It was also observed on the video that Eddie had Madeleine's "cuddle cat" in his mouth and tossed it uninterested into the air, and it was not until after the toy was actually taken to another part of the apartment and hidden from the dog, that he actually decides to give a positive alert. The report asks why if the so-called "scent of death" was on 'cuddle cat' why didn't Eddie the cadaver dog, indicate this positive immediately? (Page 2099 of the official report).

Also said *'we must also take into attention the results of the forensic analysis that was performed by the experts on the Scientific Police Laboratory on the day immediately after the facts, and already mentioned where no vestige of blood was found.'* Which we take to mean that nothing could be done about the sniffer dogs alerts because no corroborating evidence was found.

- Eddie was allowed to pass every other car, spending a total of approximately between 15 and 35 seconds on each car.
- When Eddie came to the McCann Hire car, his handler Martin Grimes kept calling Eddie back to the car for around 3.5 minutes.
- The dog kept running off completely uninterested in the car, despite sniffing at it several times.
- The dog is seen more animated in between two cars, the hire car and another, yet no providence was attached to taking Eddie to the other car, he was forced

to keep returning to the hire car until he gave a positive sign.

- The handler Martin Grimes knew that this was the hire car because it had 'find Madeleine' stickers on the windows.
- When Eddie finally indicated a positive on the car seal of 'rubber', Grimes was heard saying to the video camera 'that as the dog had indicated, he did not intend putting the dog inside the car.'
- Keela was the dog put inside the boot of the hire car NOT Eddie, she also showed no interest and tried to jump out of the boot, but was made to stay in and finally she indicated by freezing and wagging the stump of her tail.
- You can tell the two dogs apart by their markings. Eddie's markings are more on the top of his back.
- Keela's markings travel much further down her sides. (This can be seen clearly in the video.)

According To Goncalo Amaral, he made Kate and Gerry McCann arguidos (suspects) on the evidence of the sniffer dogs, even though at the time Mr Amaral did this, he knew there was no evidence on which to the charge the McCanns. Yet they were kept as official suspects for 10 months.

On Sept 15th 2007, a new procedural penal code in Portugal, was introduced making it necessary for there to be evidence against the citizen before they could be made an arguido. This was just 8 days AFTER Goncalo Amaral went to the prosecutor and asked for Kate and Gerry McCann to be made arguidos. (Official suspects)

The British sniffer dogs were not brought into the investigation until 3 months AFTER Madeleine disappeared.

The apartment where Madeleine disappeared from was not cordoned off or kept locked and secured and was not guarded at all times by a police guard after the McCann's had moved out.

Shortly after the McCanns moved out of apartment 5a, it was re-let to other holiday makers. No one knows if their DNA was taken, tested and ruled out of the investigation, no one knows if their occupations were recorded, in order to try and make sense out of the unusually conflicting evidence coming out of the apartment and so long, after Madeleine disappeared and her family moving out of apartment 5a.

It has to be said and in fact could not be disproved that many people could have inadvertently contaminated apartment 5a in the months that followed Madeleine's disappearance. Astonishingly Goncalo Amaral, then the lead detective in the Madeleine case, allowed other family's on holiday to stay in this apartment, the scene of one of the most baffling crimes in the world! In fact anyone wishing to pervert the course of justice and divert attention away from themselves or towards innocent people, could have had ample time in which to plant evidence in this very insecure holiday apartment. Amazingly, the apartment apparently still has not had its locks changed and certainly did not in the months after Madeleine's disappearance. A report in the British newspaper the 'News of the World', reported actually hiring out apartment 5a and took several pictures from inside, one was of the key to the front door, where the abductor[s] could have entered. The key was apparently studied by an independent locksmith, who confirmed this "security key" was in fact a copy! How many copies of this key are in existence? How many people who worked for Mark Warner Ocean Complex had access to this key?

Simply put, there are so many people who could have had both legitimate and illegitimate access to apartment 5a and in fact evidence could have easily been planted, which the dogs later did or did not find! It simply cannot be ruled out.

The scent of death "supposedly" detected by the cadaver dog 'Eddie', could have been manufactured. It is not clear if this manufactured scent is made anywhere in Portugal.

When dogs are trained, the smell of the pseudo cadaverine scent has to be placed in rubber balls that have virtually NO scent of rubber, this would suggest that rubber masks the scent of cadeverine or confuses the dog.

It was noted on the video that 'Eddie' the cadaver dog, supposedly indicated the scent of a cadaver at the car door 'RUBBER' seal. Yet Martin Grimes bizarrely thinks that there is no need to 'put the dog (Eddie) inside the car'.

There is a chemical company in St.Louis in the United States, that actually manufactures pseudo scents, produced to train search and rescue dogs and these scents come in several different categories, up until the production of these scents, dogs had to be trained by being indoctrinated with cadavers. The use of pig meat is also used in the training of cadaver dogs. Dogs also alert to saliva and saliva has been known to confuse cadaver dogs as it gives off a scent similar to cadaverine.

It would be very interesting to learn just how Eddie and Keela have been trained and what scents were used to train them, this could give some indication to what they would naturally alert to. Unlike real dead people, these pseudo scents, smell only to dogs. It should be noted here that no human has ever detected the smell of a dead body in the case of Eddie alerting in the Madeleine McCann case. Not in the hire car, apartment 5a or the villa and not on any of the clothes or cuddle cat.

Interestingly, children dribble, we know that saliva gives off a scent similar to cadaverine, and apparently putrescine and cadaverine are present in saliva. In the video in the car park where Eddie is seen indicating a positive to a child's T-shirt;

1. All children dribble, especially teething two year olds and as well as this, saliva quite often gets on to the clothes of toddlers and children.
2. The tea shirt that Eddie is seen indicating a positive to and tossing in the air, is NOT Madeleine's T-shirt, it does in fact belong to Sean, her two year old brother.

There are serious flaws in the lead detective's investigative prowess. The question must be asked of Goncalo Amaral, 'if he felt so strongly that the McCanns were involved, why did he allow them to drive their hire car in for examination on the day the sniffer dogs were to be put to the cars?'

Goncalo Amaral also arranged this supposedly "scientific test' in a public car park! No thought was given to if the car park was contaminated, or what smells and scents were already in the car park. No record exists of what cars were parked in the spaces before the control cars were placed there for the test, if they were vans, work cars, what kind of work they were used for, butchers, grocers, undertakers etc.

The McCanns hire car was known to all the people involved in the test, including Martin Grimes, Eddie's handler. It could not be missed because the hire car was the only silver Renault there and it still had 'Find Madeleine' stickers all over it. It has been noted that Grimes only allowed Eddie a few seconds on the other cars, yet repeatedly called Eddie back to this car until he indicated. Would Grimes have done this if he was NOT told which was the McCann hire car? Or if there was more than one silver Renault in the test and the 'Find Madeleine' stickers had been removed, thus neutralising the car's appearance?

It must also be mentioned that Eddie did give more than a passing interest in the car which was next in line to the McCanns hire car and Eddie was seen running around in circles between the two cars, yet all the attention was given to the McCann car because it was known and the other car was never examined, who did this car belong to? Should this in the name of fairness been examined? Why didn't Grimes insist that Eddie be brought back to this car repeatedly, the same as he insisted Eddie was returned to the McCann hire car?

Please note also that Martin Grimes is no longer a policeman, he is a retired policeman and now owns his own consultancy business, where they hire out Eddie and Keela's services to police forces in different countries etc.

Eddie was used in the Jersey case and indicated a positive that turned out to be a lump of old cardboard, no forensic matter was discovered in that case either.

Goncalo Amaral has said that these dogs have never given a false sign in 200 cases. So how does Goncalo Amaral explain the false positive in Jersey?

In another similar case in the United States, a judge ruled out the evidence of sniffer dogs, saying they were 'no more reliable than the flip of a coin?'

Referring back to the scent of cadaver, if the dogs did detect this and I say 'IF' because of course these are dogs and no one knows beyond reasonable doubt what they are actually sniffing, if anything at all.

The policeman that drove the McCann hire car (without overalls) to its place in the car park, is there a possibility he had come into contact with a deceased person, had any of the officers come into any contact with drowned bodies, prior to this assignment?

Goncalo Amaral himself had a pet dog who had died and for the record, it should be recorded if he had touched this dog in any way and was he wearing the same clothes? Did Amaral sit in the hire car at any time? Has the background been taken of all those that actually touched the key fob to the hire car?

Since publishing his book Goncalo Amaral was quoted in a newspaper as saying that "Gerry buried Madeleine on the beach". If this was so why did the sniffer dogs not react to any of Gerry's clothes and only supposedly reacted to Kate's? It is well known that Kate has a check-able alibi for her clothes possibly having the scent of cade-verine on them. For people who do not realise it, when a doctor certifies a dead body they do have to touch the body and do a brief examination, so Kate's explanation is actually more than plausible, it is entirely feasible.

Out of the DNA which has supposedly been found in the apartment and car after the dogs had been in, this DNA was not conclusive and could have come from Madeleine, Amelie or Kate, there is some reports that say this was mitochondrial DNA, if it was, then this could have come from any female in the McCann family.

It appears that Goncalo Amaral misinterpreted the DNA evidence from the FSS in Birmingham UK AND that from the Portuguese forensic science lab, yet still went ahead and made the parents suspects on little or no evidence.

Goncalo Amaral apparently ignored the email from John Lowe of the FSS in Birmingham, three days BEFORE he made the McCanns arguidos. The email from John Lowe gave warning that the DNA samples were inconclusive and in fact results clearly showed that these samples could belong to half the population? Knowing this Goncalo Amaral and the Portuguese prosecutor still proceeded to make The McCanns arguidos.

The British FSS made it clear that the test results were inconclusive, and should in no way form part of any investigation. Yet three days later, Goncalo Amaral lied to Gerry McCann, telling him the results were 100% positive and the McCanns were made arguidos and just 8 days later On Sept 15th 2007, a new procedural penal code in Portugal, was introduced making it necessary for

there to be evidence against the citizen before they could
be made an arguido.

13. STOP PRESS!

As we have mentioned, elsewhere in the book, the first police chief in charge of the investigation into Madeleine's abduction, Goncalo Amaral, is currently on trial in Portugal, charged with complicity in, and the covering up off, the alleged torture of Leonor Cipriano, the mother of still missing Joana. We of the Justice for ALL the McCann family forum have, naturally, been following the trial, via our Portuguese posters, with great interest. Indeed, one of the authors of this book is often in contact with Leonor's solicitor, Marcos Aragão Correia. He has already kindly supplied us with several photographs for our book, some of which have previously never been published, including the one of Joana, below.

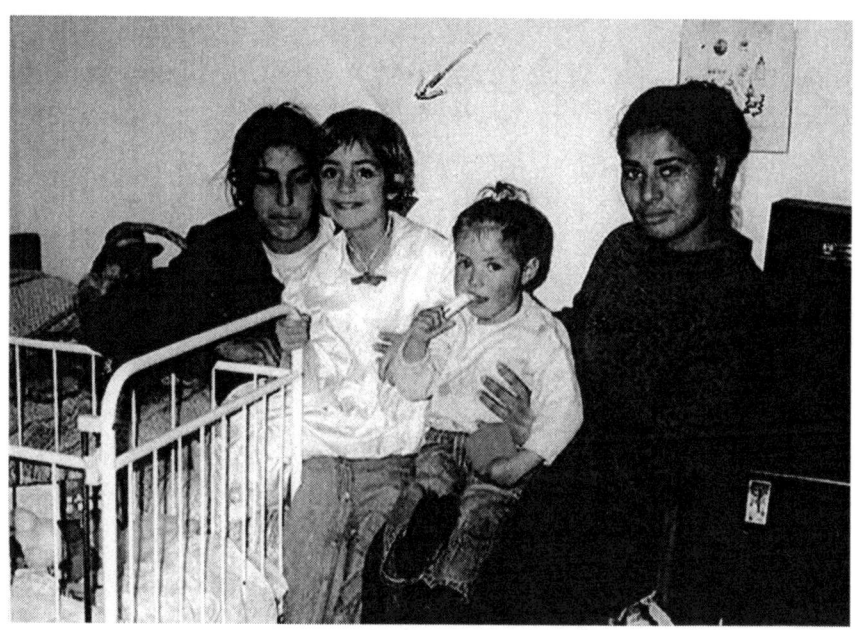

During this trial, it was alleged that Mr Amaral's wife, Sofia, left him, and the family home, and lodged a formal complaint with the police for drunken abuse and beating her up. Mr Amaral, in court and under oath, strenuously denied this, and in addition his wife withdrew the allegations, and further, denied ever making the formal complaint in the first place. There were suspicions that Sofia had received some sort of threat, in order for her to withdraw her original complaint, so as to weaken the prosecution's case on behalf of Ms Cipriano against Mr Amaral, but until now there seemed to be little hard evidence that Sofia did indeed ever make the accusation.

Until now! Quite literally as this book was at the publisher's, awaiting finalisation before going to print, Leonor's solicitor, Mr Correia, sent us some copies of documents that he had just received himself, and which he intends to produce in court. He has given us his full permission to do whatever we wish with these documents, and we thought it appropriate to include them in this book, before passing them on to the British press. What a scoop!

Now we must stress in the clearest possible terms that, though we consider Mr Correia a highly reputable source, we ourselves can in no way guarantee the authenticity of these documents, and so cannot make any hard and fast assumptions as to what they mean, or the implications that they may have for the continuing trial of Mr Amaral. However, IF they are genuine, then the first document appears to be the original letter of complaint from Sofia Amaral, wherein she alleges Goncalo, in a drunken rage, threatened to kill her. It also seems to accuse him of driving police cars while under the influence of alcohol, (Something other witnesses can verify, see the article from the Daily Mirror, where Mr Amaral is seen to consume considerable amounts of wine and beer during his two to three hour lunch breaks, before driving off, sometimes to pick his daughter up from school)

This first document is reproduced below, with an English translation beneath. (We should point out that our translator is Portuguese, so the grammar may not be perfect!)

Alexandra Sofia de Sousa Manjua Leal

Exmo. Senhor
Dr. Guilhermino Encarnação
Dignmo. Director Nacional Adjunto Da Polícia Judiciária
Directoria de Faro

Faro, 23/12/2007

Exmo. Senhor,

Como é do V/ conhecimento, sou casada com o Coordenador de Investigação Criminal, Gonçalo de Sousa Amaral, de quem tenho uma filha menor, de 4 anos, a Inês Sofia. Sabe também V.Exa. que a Inês Sofia se encontra temporariamente a residir com o pai. Venho por este meio expôr:

1. Conforme acordado com o meu marido, a Inês Sofia passaria as festas natalícias comigo, a partir da última 5ª feira, dia 20. Neste dia contactei o Gonçalo por telemóvel e fui informada de que a Inês estava, juntamente com ele, em viagem para Coimbra e só voltariam no dia seguinte;

2. Na 6ª feira, dia 21, liguei novamente ao meu marido, por volta da hora do almoço. Informou-me que estavam em viagem e que quando chegasse a Faro me entregaria a Inês. Aguardei até ás 20:00 horas sem qualquer notícia e sem que o Gonçalo atendesse o telefone. Dirigi-me então ao café perto dessa Directoria, onde encontrei o meu marido a consumir bebidas alcoólicas, juntamente com outros colegas. Tendo-lhe perguntado pela Inês Sofia, respondeu, visivelmente embriagado, que "está a descansar" e que me entregaria a menor no dia seguinte. Seguidamente ausentou-se ao volante de um veículo automóvel, marca audi, propriedade dessa instituição;

3. No Sábado, dia 22, e após inúmeras tentativas, o meu marido atendeu o telefone a meio da tarde e pediu-me que fosse buscar a Inês a casa. Dirigi-me prontamente para a residência, onde não se encontrava ninguém. O Gonçalo chegou passado algum tempo, ao volante da mesma viatura e novamente em visível estado de embriaguez. Tendo-lhe perguntado pela Inês Sofia, mandou-me entrar em casa, onde me insultou e ameaçou de morte. Abandonei o local;

4. Hoje, Domingo, dia 23, e apesar de inúmeras tentativas, o Gonçalo não atendeu o telefone e não se encontra na residência;

Infelizmente, esta situação não é acto único e isolado, e sabe V.Exa. de outras vezes em que me tenho socorrido da V/ inestimável ajuda. É neste sentido que venho solicitar-lhe que, mais uma vez, e na garantia da integridade da Inês Sofia, possa ajudar-me na sua localização.
Com os melhores cumprimentos,

185

Alexandra Sofia de Sousa Manjua Leal

Excellency
Dr. Guilhermino Encarnação
Faro's Director of the Judiciary Police

Faro, 23/12/2007

Dear Sir:

As you know I'm the wife of the Coordinator of Criminal Investigation Gonçalo Amaral, with whom I have a daughter minor of age, with 4 years old, named Inês Sofia. You know also that Inês Sofia is living temporarily with her father.

By the present way I want to expose to you:

1. As agreed with my husband, Inês Sofia should spend Christmas with me, since last Thursday, day 20th. In that day, I contacted Gonçalo by mobile phone, and I was informed that Inês was with him, in trip to Coimbra and would only return on the following day;
2. On Friday 21st, I called again my husband, around lunch time. He informed me they were still on trip and at soon he arrive to Faro he will give me Inês. I waited until 8 PM without any news and Gonçalo never answered my phone calls. I then decided to go to a pub where I encountered Gonçalo and other colleagues of him consuming alcoholic beverages, asking him by Inês Sofia, he answered, visible drunken, that "she was resting" and that he will give me the child the following day. Then he departed, driving an Audi car from the police.

3. On Saturday 22nd , and after many attempts, my husband finally answered the phone in the middle of the afternoon, and asked me to get Inês in home. I rushed to the residence, but nobody was there. After a while, Gonçalo appeared driving the same car, and again in a notorious state of drunkenness. Having asked him for Inês Sofia, he ordered me to go inside the house, where he insulted me and threatened me of death. I abandoned the place.
4. Today, Sunday 23rd, and after numerous attempts, Gonçalo never answered his phone and he is not at home.

Unfortunately, this situation is not a unique and isolated act, and you Sir well know about other times in the past where I've also asked for your help. Once more, I ask again for your help, in order to guarantee Inês Sofia integrity, and in order to localize her.

Best Regards,

Alexandra Sofia de Sousa Manjua Leal

The next document is a daily log, filled out to show the day's activities. As you can see, it clearly shows in item 6 the receipt of the official complaint form from Sofia Amaral. Together with the first document, if these are genuine, then it proves that Sofia DID INDEED lodge a formal complaint of violence, and the report confirms that the police DID INDEED receive it. The English is below, followed by the original document.

STAND BY TEAM REPORT
Sunday, 23rd of December 2007

1. STAND BY TEAM

1.1 C.i.C. Amável de Sousa
1.2 Team Leader: Salvado dos Santos, Inspector
1.3 Inspectors: Nuno Peixe
1.4 Lofoscopistas:
1.5 Others:
(Indicate name and category)

2. COMPOSITION CHANGES
2.1 ABSENCES AND SUBSTITUTIONS
2.2 LEAVES

Nothing to record

2.3 REINFORCEMENTS

Around 08:40 Inspector Paulo Silvestre and Adjoin-Specialist Henrique Vieira were called so that they make judiciary inspections to fires that took place in Olhão, having finished the task by 11:00.-----------

3.BUILDING

(List shifts, round inspections [don't know a better expression], keys, people and vehicle movements, flags, break downs, etc - whenever they are not tasks assured by other services)

.   Stand by vehicle: 09-79-QM
.   Shifts: 00:00 - 04:15 - Salvado Santos
    04:15 - 08:30 - Nuno Peixe

4 ARGUIDOS' MOUVEMENTS
4.1 DETAINEES IN AND OUT
4.2 ARGUIDOS PERIODICAL PRESENTATIONS
[show up]

5. PREVENTION UNITS
(Mention effective service, called employees, reason, calling time, beginning and end)

- Inspectors: Carlos Minga (SRCB), Carlos Guerreiro (SICCP) and Paulo Silvestre.
- Technical [forensic???] police: Henrique Viera [probably Vieira]

6. OCCURRENCIES
6.1 INTERNAL

(Summary of received denunciations and communications and informations compiled by the services)

. Thirty kilograms of haxixe [cannabis, I believe] were handed by the Maritime Police of Olhão apprehended under NUIPC 81/07.6MAOLH, according to handing document, which were deposited in this Directory's vault.

A letter addressed to the Adjoin-National Director, lic Guilhermino da Encarnação was handed to this stand by team by Mrs. Alexandra Sofia de Sousa Manjua Leal.

6.2 EXTERNAL
(Report of facts occurring during execution of outside diligences)

- One prevention team went to Olhão where it made forensic inspections in several streets in the city where, in the morning [dawn] of the 23rd December, several fires erupted in garbage containers of which resulted fires in several vehicles parked in the vicinity.

6.3 OTHERS

Faro, 24th December 2007

S R

MINISTÉRIO DA JUSTIÇA

POLÍCIA JUDICIÁRIA

DIRECTORIA FARO

RELATÓRIO DO SERVIÇO DE PIQUETE

Domingo, 23 de Dezembro de 2007

1. COMPOSIÇÃO DO PIQUETE

1.1 C.i.C.: Lic. Amável de Sousa

1.2 Chefe de piquete: Salvado dos Santos, Inspector

1.3 Inspectores: Nuno Peixe

1.4 Lofoscopistas:

1.5 Outros:

(indicar nome e categoria)

2. ALTERAÇÕES NA COMPOSIÇÃO

2.1 FALTAS E SUBSTITUIÇÕES

☐ -

2.2 DISPENSAS

☐ - nada a registar.

2.3 REFORÇOS

☐- Cerca das 8H40 foi chamado o Inspector Paulo Silvestre e o Especialista-Adjunto Henrique Vieira a fim de efectuarem inspecções judiciárias a incêndios ocorridos em Olhão, tendo terminado o serviço pelas 11H00. -------

3. EDIFÍCIO

(mencionar turnos, rondas, chaves, movimentos de pessoas e viaturas, bandeiras, avarias, etc. - sempre que não sejam tarefas asseguradas por outros serviços)

• Viatura de piquete: 09-79-QM

•Turnos: 00H00 - 04H15 - Salvado Santos

04H15 - 08H30 - Nuno Peixe

4. MOVIMENTO DE ARGUIDOS

4.1 ENTRADA E SAÍDA DE PRESOS

5. UNIDADES DE PREVENÇÃO
(mencionar serviço efectivo, funcionários convocados, motivo, hora da convocatória, do início e fim)

☐ - Inspectores: Carlos Minga (SRCB), Carlos Guerreiro (SICCP) e Paulo Silvestre.
☐ - Polícia Técnica: Henrique Viera

6. OCORRÊNCIAS

6.1 INTERNAS
(súmula de denúncias e comunicações recebidas e informações e diligências pelo serviço)

• Foram entregues pela Polícia Marítima de Olhão trinta quilogramas de estupefaciente haxixe apreendidos no âmbito do NUIPC 81/07.6MAOLH, conforme termo de entrega, os quais foram depositados no cofre forte desta Directoria.
• Foi entregue uma carta aberta neste piquete pela senhora Alexandra Sofia de Sousa Manjua Leal dirigida ao senhor Director-Nacional Adjunto, Ilc Guilhermino da Encarnação.

6.2 EXTERNAS
(relato de ocorrências de factos com realização de diligências no exterior)

• Uma equipa da prevenção deslocou-se à cidade de Olhão onde efectuou inspecções judiciárias em diversas ruas desta cidade, nas quais, na madrugada do dia 23 de Dezembro do corrente, ocorreram diversos incêndios em contentores do lixo de que terão resultado a propagação de incêndios em várias viaturas estacionadas nas proximidades.

6.3 DIVERSAS

•

Faro, 24 de Dezembro de 2007	
O C.I.C. DE PIQUETE assinatura nome por extenso: Amiável de Sousa	O CHEFE DE PIQUETE assinatura nome por extenso: Salvado Santos

192

So, what does this mean? Well, IF these are genuine documents, this would show the character of the man, painting a picture of a violent, misogynistic, abusive alcoholic, prone to drinking heavily while on duty, driving police cars while under the influence of alcohol, and even endangering the life of his own daughter during his bouts of drink driving. Sofia has had her life threatened, and not, it seems, for the first time, and is clearly concerned for the safety of their daughter.

But, most importantly of all, they would go to prove that Mr Amaral has lied under oath in a court of law. This begs the question, what else is he prepared to lie about? What else is he covering up, and who for? The man's incompetence, as far as the investigation goes, is already established beyond any reasonable doubt, but we have to ask the question, is he, in fact, corrupt? If he is indeed prepared to use torture in order to secure a conviction, even without any evidence, of an innocent woman, is he then capable of lying in the McCann case? Is he capable, willing even, to break his own countries so-called strict secrecy laws and spread slurs and lies about the parents, to discredit them in the eyes of the public, in order to secure yet another unjust conviction?

These documents are damning evidence, and if they are genuine, and we have no reason to suspect otherwise, then it must be said that Mr Amaral was not fit to be in charge of the investigation into Madeleine's abduction, and now, more than ever, the argument for a full and open public enquiry is unassailable.

14. POACHER TURNED GAMEKEEPER?

From 'Justice for ALL McCann family' forum.

I can't get my head around this!

Portugal used to have a child agency called 'Institute de Apolo a Crianca' which published details of and looked for missing children.

http://minnea.blogspot.com/

There is now a new set up, a new organisation specialising in missing children called: **Portuguese Association for missing Children.**

Brilliant! I thought.

Then I saw who was leading this brand new Organisation for Missing Children - our friend, **Paulo Pereira Christovao is President.**

- Yes,the same Paulo Christovao accused of Torture in the ongoing Cipriano Torture Trial. One of the men thought to have falsely accused Leanor of murder, rather than do a proper search for Joana – a missing child
- The man who was a Chief Inspector, with Amaral and others who failed to find missing children. Who gave up too early and who accused others (who are now thought innocent) of the crimes.
- The man who as a journalist is suspected of releasing all the deliberately incriminating disinformation about the McCanns, courtesy of his friend and ex-colleague Goncalo Amaral. Am I correct in thinking that they are both **dismissed** ex PJ Chief Inspectors?
- The man who has made money from missing children, by releasing two books. One book about Joana Cipriano, the other about Madeleine McCann

The man who says that the Organisation was founded to find eight missing children – BUT NOT MADELEINE! He said this to 24Horas. But not Madeleine because the McCanns are suspects!

http://www.dailymail.co.uk/news/article-501093/McCanns-arrested-abandoning-Madeleine-missing-childrens-boss-says.html

No doubt both these books are full of the same disinformation as his newspaper articles were. Is this what is called 'Paedo Tom-Tom'?

What's going on? So this man who couldn't be bothered to do a proper search for a missing child (preferring the culprit to get away?), who deliberately released disinformation (paedo tom-tom?) to incriminate the mother (preferring the abductor to get away?) and who wrote two books making money from the missing children is **leading** a new organisation specialising in missing children called, 'The Portuguese Association for Missing Children'! What is going on?

Why is a man who seems to be against finding missing children, running an organisation such as this? Why would such a man want to run such an organisation? Who would appoint him to such a position? What I am asking myself is - does he have an ulterior motive? Does the person who appointed him have an ulterior motive? Do you get what I am driving at?

PORTUGAL. **WAKE UP!** WHAT IS GOING ON?

As I said, I can't get my head around this!

15. Mr Bennett's 'Reasons.'

Now we come to the second raison d'être for the existence of our volume, where we discuss the literary skills of one Anthony Bennett, solicitor, (Retd.)

Mr Bennett, for reasons we have often discussed on our forum, but are only truly known to himself, took it upon himself to write a book, and call it "What really happened to Madeleine McCann? 60 reasons that suggest she was not abducted." In addition, Mr Bennett has a website set up to promote not only his book, but an organisation he has set up, called 'The Madeleine foundation.' On this website he sets out clear goals, one of which is to attempt to bring a private prosecution against Kate and Gerry McCann for neglect, despite the fact that there is, was, and never has been any evidence to show that any of the McCann children were ever neglected. The Foundation, the website and the book are all tools to be used in achieving this goal, but it is the book which is by far the most dangerous part of this triumvirate, and that is why we feel the need to comprehensively take it apart, and show it for the work of poisonous fiction it actually is.

On Mr Bennett's website there is a condensed version of the book, laying out the first thirty of his so called 'reasons' and since not one of us on the forum would dirty ourselves by buying a full copy of his book, we will deal only with these first thirty. But in truth we really need not even bother with that many. If even one part of one reason is clearly shown to be flawed, false or inaccurate, then the whole book fails. As someone famous once said, "One has only to kick in the front door, and the whole rotten structure will come crashing to the ground!" We can do no better than start with this, part of his fourteenth reason, ignoring advice not to highlight Madeleine's 'coloboma' eye defect.

All the McCanns' publicity posters strongly emphasized the coloboma, placing Madeleine at even greater risk. They even trade-marked Madeleine's coloboma.

The legend about the parents trade marking of Madeleine's coloboma, in a supposed cynical attempt to 'cash in' on her disappearance was one of the very first myths to spring up in the early days of the abduction, and still seems to have a certain provenance it doesn't deserve. All it would have taken to either confirm or discredit this particular fable was to actually go on the official British Trademark website, and contact them. This we did, and this was the e-mail we got back, less than twelve hours later.

Dear **********,

Thank you for contacting us.

Marcaria.com is an international company that deals with every aspect of registration and protection of trademarks and domains with presence in the main countries of America, Europe, Asia, Africa and Oceania. Marcaria. com has experienced intellectual property attorneys in each country who are personally in charge of the requested services.

Regarding your question please note that it is our understanding **that it is not possible to trademark a body part.**

In case you want to register a Copyright, trademark or domain name, please don't hesitate in contacting me.

Best regards,

Francisca Zambrano
Manager - Patentarea.com
www.patentarea.com
<u>www.marcaria.com</u>

It is not possible to trade mark a body part. That, from the official body who know better than anyone what is or is not possible with regards trade marking. But Mr. Bennett failed completely to even undertake this quick and easy double-check before including it in his book, and attempting to pass it off as fact. As we said earlier, if even one of Mr. Bennett's reasons fails to stand up to scrutiny, then his whole book itself must come under question. This one example of the abject failure of Mr. Bennett to carry out even the simplest of checks we feel sets the standard for the rest of Mr. Bennett's research, or, to be more precise, the complete lack of it.

As an aside, to further show Mr. Bennett's dubious integrity, if you look on his Madeleine Foundation website, he quotes at length from the website of the National Society for the Prevention of Cruelty to Children. It would seem, at first glance, that he is suggesting he has the backing of the NSPCC in his 'crusade.' So, once again we decided to check up on what Mr. Bennett is trying to have us believe. We contacted the NSPCC, explaining that Mr. Bennett seemed to be exploiting their views, and insinuating that they somehow were behind him. We felt it nessecary to carry out this check, because it seems that Mr. Bennett cannot be trusted to be completely open and honest with us, either in his book OR on his website. And it seems, once again, we were right. The NSPCC in fact catagorically DENIED that they were in any way aware of Mr Bennett, his website or his book, and went to great lengths to assure us that they most certainly did NOT support his views with regard to the McCann's.

So, it would now seem, beyond any reasonable doubt, that Mr Bennett is at best discredited as any kind of source of reliable information regarding the Madeleine case, and at worst, could even be considered a fraud. We could probably stop right here, as the point has been conclusivly made. But, as we said earlier, Mr Bennett and his book represent far too big a threat to Madeleine, and the ongoing search for her, to take any chances. The risks he poses to Madeleine's safety are just too great. So we must go further, go the extra mile, to make sure that as many people as possible realise just how far from the truth Mr. Bennett really is, because the alternative is to simply give up on Madeleine, and that is something the members of this forum will never contemplate. So at this point, we thought it best to simply show you some of the conversations that have taken place within our forum, with regards to Mr. Bennett's pathetic so called 'reasons that suggest she was not abducted.' One of our members has written a separate section, specifically about the sheer imposibility of a cover up, as suggested by Mr Bennett. Finally we will finish with a brief list of the first thirty reasons, interspersed with a few final points of our own.

16. THE SHEER IMPOSIBILITY.

In Tony Bennett's book, '60 reasons,' one rationale he believes suggests that there was no abduction is, in his opinion, it's sheer impossibility. Using fanciful and unfounded ideas, he attempts to persuade his readers that the abduction theory is untenable. This, he deduces, can only mean one thing; Madeleine 'probably' died in the apartment and her parents then covered up the fact. We would like now to take the opportunity to rubbish this viewpoint, and point out the sheer impossibility of such a cover up.

Firstly, if Madeleine died, as claimed, in the apartment, we need to look at the probable cause of death. Mr Amaral, in *his* book, 'The truth of the lie' suggests at least two, the first being that she died of an accidental overdose of 'Capal, a sleeping drug.' We believe he means Calpol, a commonly administered child medication, readily available in any high street chemists. But had Mr Amaral been a detective of any reasonable calibre, he would have done his homework, and discovered that Calpol is NOT a 'sleeping drug.' It in fact has NO sedative properties whatsoever. Calpol is an antipyretic, designed to reduce fever. If your child has a temperature, and you give them a dose of Calpol, it helps to reduce the child's temperature, thus allowing them to fall asleep naturally, not because of any ingredients in the Calpol itself. Also, the manufacturers are well aware of the dangers of children finding and swallowing interesting bottles of yummy looking liquids, and so only sell Calpol in bottles of a size too small to offer any serious danger to a child swallowing the entire contents. Strike one.

The other reason suggested is that she died as the result of a fall, possibly from climbing on the sofa after the parents went for their evening meal. If that was the case, we then need to discuss Kate's reaction on discovering her daughter, dead, on the floor. We know what ours would be, and we can probably imagine yours. But let's imagine, if we can, Kate's, and to get a better idea of what that may be we need to go back in time, back to before Madeleine was born, to her time of conception. As most readers know, Madeleine was born via I.V.F, as were her twin siblings. If you were fortunate enough to have been able to conceive naturally and easily, you may not know how emotional and distressing, the process of I.V.F. can be. If, on the other hand, you HAVE been through the I.V.F. process, you hardly need us to tell you. Indeed, it is usually considered as the last resort of couples who are so desperate to have a child, that they would consider anything, however stressful, rather than remain childless. Let us repeat that, couples who are DESPERATE to have a child. As a result, many paediatric psychiatrists claim that the bond between a mother and child conceived this way goes much further and deeper than one formed from a natural conception. And yet Mr Amaral would have us believe that Kate's first reaction upon finding her daughter dead is something like, "Oh Damn, how am I going to clean THIS mess up?"

But let's follow Mr Amaral's flawed thinking further. Before raising the alarm, by screaming in a supposedly 'pretend' panic, she would have first needed to hide the body. WHERE? We are not willing for one second to just blindly accept that she "hid' the body, 'somewhere." We want to know WHERE. We want to know a plausible hiding place, given the short amount of time Kate had at her disposal. It couldn't have been in the flat, as that was searched, not only by the friends, but the first GNR on the scene. And please don't mention the freezer, the average holiday flat kitchen freezer is just about big enough for a packet of frozen peas. She would have been unlikely to think of putting the body in the dustbins, because logically, that would have been the first place a sensible person would have looked. She couldn't have believed that the GNR and the PJ would be so incompetent as to forgo even searching the bins, before allowing the bins to be emptied within a few days of the abduction, so Kate would have almost certainly ruled that out. It would also be unlikely she hid Madeleine somewhere outside. As a tourist, not a resident, she would have little idea, if any, of the layout of the local area, or where would be a good hiding place. (When YOU go on holiday, do you subconsciously keep a lookout for good places to hide YOUR child's body, 'just in case?') So then, the second fundamental flaw in Mr Amaral's theory, after cause of death, is, where did Kate hide the body?

What would have happened next? Well, if we imagine that somehow Kate DID manage to hide the body, she would have had to break the news to Gerry. Gerry, remember, was back at the Tapas restaurant at the time of the alarm being raised. During the commotion and panic, Kate would have had to try to find a quiet moment to take Gerry aside and tell him, "Look, I'm so sorry, Madeleine wasn't abducted, I found her dead on the floor. I hid her for now, but we need to maintain this abduction pretence." What do you suppose HIS reaction would have been? Finding out his daughter is not just missing, but actually dead? OK, he would already be hugely upset, but don't you think he would have yelled at Kate in some way? With all the people coming and going, wouldn't someone have seen or heard this? These are two ordinary people, who in their entire lives have never once raised an ounce of suspicion from their neighbours or friends, and yet they are able to control their emotions over the death of their much longed for and greatly loved daughter in such a way that nobody doubted them even for a second? Do YOU really believe that?

Now to the friends, the so-called 'Tapas seven.' At least one, and possibly all of whom Mr Amaral suspects helped the parents to dispose of the body to a better hiding place, and assist in the cover up. All sworn to a pact of secrecy. Just suppose, even for a second, Kate and Gerry WERE able to control themselves long enough to conceal the body, and concoct a cover story. We now have to accept Mr Amaral's suggestion that all of the friends agreed to go along with this story. We must ask you, what are the chances of ALL of them agreeing to this? We would have thought that at least one of them would have said, "Look, we sympathise with you completely, we feel just as devastated over Maddie's death as you do, but you must tell the truth. You can't expect to get away with it forever, the truth will come out eventually. If you don't admit what happened now, it will only be much worse for you later when the police eventually find it out themselves." Surely one, if not more, of the friends would have acted as the voice of reason? Mr Amaral's theory is now beginning to unravel faster than a ball of wool in a room full of kittens.

But why would they want to cover up her death in the first place? The McCann's are on record as stating that when they booked their holiday they believed the resort ran a 'drop-in' nanny service, where a maid or nanny patrolled the resort, listening in, or opening the door and checking, on all children of families who paid for this service. Such listening or drop-in services are still widely used across the U.K. and Europe, and it was in fact available at the resort they stayed at the previous year. After assuming they would be able to use such a service at Praia de Luz, they were surprised to find it not available after all. So instead they made their own arrangements, to copy the service for themselves. There were enough of them, so that each one of the friends would only have needed to make one visit, check on all of their children, then return to the table for their meal. The staff at the resort are on record as saying many other families did the same that summer, not just the McCann's and their friends. Kate and Gerry, while being interviewed, have told us that while they deeply regretted their decision now, at the time they thought their actions were within the bounds of reasonable parenting. If that is the case, then they would have had nothing to fear from admitting that Madeleine suffered an accident while she was alone between visits. So far then, no motive, no cause of death, no body. Cover up? It just doesn't make sense.

But there is also another theory, propounded by the inhabitants of the more hate promoting internet forums, and this is as good a time as any to discuss it. This one speculates that Madeleine died, accidentally or otherwise, earlier that day, before the parents even went out for their evening meal. This means we now have to consider the proposition that two clearly loving parents, of which one, Kate, is known to be painfully shy, were able to calmly dispose of their daughter's body, then go for a meal and laugh and joke as if nothing had happened. They would have to have put on an act worthy of an Oscar, all without raising the slightest suspicion. But if that was indeed the case, if there was any attempt at a cover up, why wait till half way through the meal before raising the alarm? Surely the best time would have been first thing the next morning, on waking up. That way there would be no danger of being under suspicion themselves. In fact, if Kate was truly the ice maiden some of the more ignorant internet bloggers would have us believe, then why, on discovering Madeleine's body, did she not just pick her up, place her back in bed, and carry on as normal? Then, in the morning, she and Gerry could return her body to the scene of the accident, and then claim she must have got out of bed in the night and had a fall, while everyone else was asleep? That way all suspicion would be removed, with the added bonus of there being no body to dispose of. No, in our opinion the whole idea of Madeleine dying before the parents left the apartment is the most ridiculous scenario of all, and we dismiss it out of hand.

However, getting back to the alleged cover up. Mr Amaral, and also Mr Bennett would have us believe the cover up goes even further. MUCH further. In fact, all the way to the very top of the British Government, and the Prime minister himself. Both allege that there is government involvement, up to and including a ministerial order to protect Kate and Gerry, and discredit the Portuguese enquiry into Madeleine's disappearance. Again, we have but one simple question. WHY? If ministers, possibly even the Prime minister, knew that Kate and Gerry had been responsible for Madeleine's demise, what possible reason could they have for getting involved in, or even ordering the cover-up of, the death, possibly murder of an innocent child? If such a thing ever got out, and such things have a habit of doing so, the damage to the reputation of all those involved would be enormous. And just who are Kate and Gerry to warrant such high level protection anyway? If we go back to the lower class forums again, they will tell you it is because the McCann's have very rich and influential friends, people with connections, able to pull strings in the highest of places. But we must ask you, in all reason, how likely is that? Gerry, the youngest of five, son of an Irish immigrant family to Scotland, who grew up in a Glasgow tenement block. Kate, who came from a working class background in Liverpool. Both of them worked very hard, studied, and became doctors. Two of thousands of doctors all over the country. Respected, yes, but hardly out of the ordinary. So how on earth did these humble medical practitioners become involved with the likes of Richard Branson and Brian Kennedy? Has any attempt been made, by any of the investigating authorities, to check out what, if any, connections the McCann's had with these powerful and well known public figures prior to the 3rd of May, 2007? NO. Because, before Madeleine was abducted, the McCann's had never met any of these high flyers, and nor would they ever, if fate had not so cruelly intervened. The truth is, all of these people, the Virgin Media boss, the millionaire building magnate, the Prime minister, all got involved for the simple reason that they had sympathy for the suffering parents of an abducted child, and wanted to show their support, either financially or politically. The simplest explanation is usually the correct one. There is no conspiracy, no government cover up, and there never was one.

But there is one final thing to consider. Imagine then, that so far to date Madeleine's body has been successfully kept hidden, the secrecy pact has so far held, the cover up has been maintained, and the police have failed to find any evidence whatsoever of the parents involvement in her disappearance. What would be the most sensible course of action to have taken, once the 'Arguido' status was lifted from the parents, and the official police documents cleared the parents of any involvement? If they were indeed guilty, we would imagine everyone involved would heave a huge sigh of relief. Kate and Gerry in particular, though mourning the loss of their daughter, would be happy with the knowledge that they had 'got away with it.' The best thing then would be to keep quiet. To slip slowly away from the public eye, doing their best to not draw any attention to themselves. Perhaps, in six months to a year after being cleared, they may make one final public statement to the effect that they had finally accepted that their daughter was gone, in all probability never to be found, and that the search was therefore going to be wound up, with all remaining cash in the Find Madeleine fund going to children's charities. But instead what do they do? They announce that they are hiring one of the best American detective agencies money can buy. They also tell everyone they are looking to hire as many retired detectives and experts in this country as they possibly can. Wouldn't you think, if they really had something to hide, they would be just the slightest bit afraid that one of these great detectives would discover their secret?

That is the greatest damnation of the cover up theory of all. Kate and Gerry are, in fact, still determined to do whatever it takes to find Madeleine, their firstborn child, their beloved daughter, and they still cling doggedly to the belief that somewhere she may just still be alive. If that were not the case, why then even bother with another Christmas video appeal, asking for any information that may have so far been forgotten?

Mr Amaral and Mr Bennett are asking us to take their word. They are asking us to trust them, to stretch our incredulity to breaking point, to reach the same conclusions. Why? Because they know better than us. Well we say, no. Not just no, but HELL no. Their whole argument can be demolished with but four simple words. No body, no proof. Until we have one or the other, we choose not to believe a single word either of you say.

17. FURTHER EVIDENCE OF MR BENNETT'S FLAWED REASONING.

The following are quotes from our own forum, between various members about Mr Bennett, and some of his 'reasons' The identities of the posters has, for obvious reasons, been blanked out.

A conversation about Mr Bennett's dubious 'statistics.'

**** said,
Just from what I have read of the contents of Tony's rag, I think he is destined for the courts.

And there is a reason that the rag is self published.

One wonders though at the mentality of people that buy the rag. What could they possible hope to get from it. It contains a number of completely unfounded allegations which he cannot prove and much of which contradicts the official PJ files.

Lets take the use of statisics for eg to 'prove' that Madeleine was not abducted. I am sure that these statistics (which are directly contradicted by the FBI's own statistics and by that of experts in this field, as proven by the Riley Fox case in the US) are great comfort to those parents whose children were abducted from their homes/baths/beds. To know that it couldnt possibley have happened, because Tony Bennett says so. So I guess those children are just missing forever.

Lets take the case of Riley Fox. It is proven in a court of law in the US that she was abducted from her home while she slept, was raped, murdered and left in the river. And it is also proven that her parents were not involved (due to DNA evidence found on her body which conclusively introduces a person who is not her father or any relative or friend of the family). This was stranger abduction and it had the worst results.

The fact is, that no one knows for certain what happened to Madeleine. There is no proof that she was murdered, or even accidentally killed in the apartment. She has not been officially declared dead. If this rag makes any accusations against the McCanns or their associates, they will see Bennett in court.

He needs to examine his motives for why he writes such stuff. He doesnt represent Madeleine, and he is doing nothing to find her or to even find out what happened to her. Making up theories based on no evidence is completely useless.

If there is no evidence of death, then how can death be assumed. There is no evidence that doesnt support an abduction. That is there is no evidence that contradicts an abduction. So therefore any evidence (or lack of it) supports an abduction. Therefore any reasonable person has to assume it is an abduction.

**** said,

Very good post, *****. I didn't know about the Riley-Fox case, but in Britain (I think you are in Australia?) we have the Peter Voisey case. If a writer of fiction ever contemplated a crime like his, the writer would lose all credibilty.

And in a post of mine about Lino Henrique, I give a another angle on the *there's no evidence of an abduction* line. For there to *be* evidence, you need a control sample of the abductor. Without the control sample, there will be no evidence.

As for the rest of Mr Bennett's book, he has it there were two cadaver dogs when there was one. And he has it that Mark Harrison advised the PJ to proceed on the basis that Madeleine died in the apartment. The assumption, in the files, was actually made by PJ officer Jaoa Carlos. I'm sure there's much more cud to chew.

**** said,

I saw your post about the DNA. I had thought along those lines myself and am glad that I am not the only one to wonder about such things. As there is DNA that hasnt been identified, how can it be ruled out as the DNA of the abductor???? It was like the so called match to Madeleine's DNA. There was no match. There was a percentage match of markers against a conglomeration of 3 different people's DNA, which many of the FSS staff also matched to, and I suspect so did half or all of the McCann family. So by stating that they cannot confirm or exclude

Madeleine's DNA is rubbish. IMO, they could exclude it based on the matching of so many others to it, that it is most likely a match based on 'statistics' as it was for all the FSS staff members.

IMO, in many cases it is not possible to prove an abduction, it is becomes the likely scenario because other scenarios are eliminated.

You are right, I am from Australia. We have had our own fair share of terrible cases, such as Azaria Chamberlain. We also had the Beaumont children (3 children who went missing from Glenelg beach in Adelaide in the 60's, never found, no bodies ever found), we had a notorious predatory paedophile who abducted children from very near to their homes and murdered them, My mum told me the other day about a little boy who was taken from our local area about 40 years ago about 4 who went to the mail box to meet the postie as he did everyday and then just disappeared, and so on. And then we have the modern cases. Most notably a little 18mo girl taken from her home in Sydney named Rahma. Here is a link to a short blurb.

http://www.mako.org.au/ausnews508.html

It is now accepted by the police that she was abducted from her bed. I have read more recent articles, and there was no forensics ever found, and the fly screen was cut from the outside but there is no evidence that the child was taken through the window etc, but she is not in the house, so she was taken out somehow. She just disappeared, never to be seen again. And as a matter of process, the parents were considered as possible suspects but were ruled out very early on, but only after a thorough investigation. As should have happened with the McCanns. And then our police tried to do their jobs properly and tried to find the child, they are still looking. There was a request for information not long ago.

This is the proper process and the abduction scenario is all that is left, as there is no evidence for any other. Exactly as with Madeleine. So tell me, why are there so many halfwits that keep insisting any different. Surely, at some point, they must realise that if the McCanns had killed Madeleine (deliberately or accidentally) that there would have been some proof in the apartment. It does always bring me back to why were the sheets off of Madeleines' bed washed. If she had died in that bed, there would have been some proof on the sheets. Why did the PJ let those sheets go to be washed? Because if those sheets were forensically examined and there was nothing to indicate any drugs, or death, then that would have instantly dispelled any overdose theories, etc etc. Even, we, as amateurs, know that the sheets should have been preserved, as should the towels, and everything from the bins, and the floor should have been forensically examined etc etc. Why didnt any of this get done? Is it just incompetence, or something more sinister.

I think Mr Bennett should question this type of thing. Because regardless of what he believes happened to Madeleine, if the crime scene had of been preserved properly and top flight forensics done, then the truth would probably be known. In fact, if Bennett were right (AS IF), then the correct forensics and procedures would most likely have proved this. Bennett should at least criticise the PJ for this.

Just as further proof of the unreliability of Mr Bennett's 'statistics', where he claims no child was ever abducted from their home, here are some cases, culled at random, from missing persons websites from around the world. Most of these children are within a few years either way of Madeleine's age, all were abducted from their home, holiday residence, or within very close proximity. All were abducted by strangers, and it is a fair bet the parents claimed their child was abducted.

REACHELLE SMITH
Aged four at time of abduction. She was last seen at her home in the early morning hours of May 17, 2006. She is missing under suspicious circumstances.

http://www.ncmec.org/missingkids/servlet/PubCaseSearchServlet?act=viewPoster&caseNum=1044761&orgPrefix=NCMC&searchLang=en_US

BRYAN DOSSANTOS-GOMES
Aged just two months when taken. Bryan was last seen in the area of Estero, Florida.

http://www.ncmec.org/missingkids/servlet/PubCaseSearchServlet?act=viewPoster&caseNum=1058972&orgPrefix=NCMC&searchLang=en_US

TRENTON DUCKETT
Two years old when abducted, He was last seen at approximately 7:00 p.m. on August 27, 2006.

http://www.missingkids.com/missingkids/servlet/PubCaseSearchServlet?act=viewPoster&caseNum=1052224&orgPrefix=NCMC&searchLang=en_US

LEEANNA WARNER

Taken at age of five. She was last seen at home at 5 p.m. on June 14, 2003.

http://208.254.21.169/missingkids/servlet/PubCaseSearchServlet?act=viewPoster&caseNum=965221&orgPrefix=NCMC&searchLang=en_US

SABRINA PAIGE AISENBERG

Disappeared as a five month old baby. She became missing from her residence sometime during the early hours of November 24th, 1997.

http://www.missingkids.com/missingkids/servlet/PubCaseSearchServlet?act=viewChildDetail&caseNum=840605&orgPrefix=NCMC&seqNum=1&caseLang=en_US&searchLang=en_US

HIBA HAMED

Seven years old at time of disappearance. Last seen 10th July, 2007.

http://uk.missingkids.com/missingkids/servlet/PubCaseSearchServlet?act=viewChildDetail&LanguageCountry=en_GB&searchLang=en_GB&caseLang=en_GB&orgPrefix=UK02&caseNum=NOTTS08082008&seqNum=1

MARY BOYLE

Abducted at just seven years old, Mary Boyle has been missing from her Grandmother's home at Ballyshannon Co Donegal, since the 18th March 1977.

http://www.missingkids.ie/missingkids/servlet/PubCaseSearchServlet?act=viewPoster&caseNum=MK1&orgPrefix=IRGS&searchLang=en_IE

JENNIFER WANG
Just over two years old at time of disappearance.

http://nl.missingkids.com/missingkids/servlet/PubCase
SearchServlet?act=viewChildDetail&LanguageCountry=
nl_NL&searchLang=nl_NL&caseLang=nl_NL&orgPrefi
x=NLZO&caseNum=06150469&seqNum=1

JEREMI JOSE VARGAS SUAREZ
**Seven year old Jeremi vanished while playing in his
front garden. His parents are convinced his abduction
is somehow linked to Madeleine's.**

http://www.icmec.com/missingkids/servlet/PubCaseSea
rchServlet?act=viewPoster&caseNum=EEG5_3261&orgP
refix=ESNI&searchLang=en_X1

GEORGINA NAGY EDIT DE VRIES
Missing since 15th July, 2007, aged ten.

http://nl.missingkids.com/missingkids/servlet/PubCase
SearchServlet?act=viewChildDetail&LanguageCountry=
nl_NL&searchLang=nl_NL&caseLang=nl_NL&orgPrefi
x=NLZO&caseNum=07020513&seqNum=1

DENISE PIPITONE
**Abducted on 1st Sept, 2004, aged just four years old,
Denise has been called in the British press the Italian
Madeleine McCann.**

http://www.icmec.com/missingkids/servlet/PubCaseSea
rchServlet?act=viewPoster&caseNum=00000047&orgPre
fix=ITRM&searchLang=en_X1

KARIM DHAHRI
Less than a year old when taken.

http://it.missingkids.com/missingkids/servlet/PubCaseS
earchServlet?act=viewPoster&caseNum=00000058&orgP
refix=ITRM&searchLang=it_IT

ANNA PSHENYCHNYAK
Under three years old when abducted.

http://it.missingkids.com/missingkids/servlet/PubCaseS
earchServlet?act=viewPoster&caseNum=00000037&orgP
refix=ITRM&searchLang=it_IT

NICOLE LOUISE MORIN
Nicole was last seen home, aged eight.

http://www.icmec.org/missingkids/servlet/PubCaseSear
chServlet?act=viewPoster&caseNum=8608792&orgPrefi
x=RCMP&searchLang=en_X1

TAMRA KEEPNESS
**Six year old Tamra disappeared from her bedroom
overnight.**

http://www.icmec.org/missingkids/servlet/PubCaseSear
chServlet?act=viewPoster&caseNum=0400547&orgPrefi
x=RCMP&searchLang=en_X1

RAHME EL-DENNAOUI
**She was last seen by her parents when she was put in
her bed at 2am on Thursday 10 November, 2005.**

http://www.icmec.com/missingkids/servlet/PubCaseSea
rchServlet?act=viewPoster&caseNum=nmpcc0001&orgP
refix=AUCB&searchLang=en_X1

We can also include the case of American Girl, Elizabeth Smart, abducted from her bedroom, but, thank God, recovered safely less than a year later some forty miles from her home.

Remember, Mr Bennett dismisses each and every one of these cases as non-existant. In his opinion, none of these children were abducted by strangers, because, according to his book, *stranger abduction just doesn't happen*. I doubt his words will bring much comfort to the parents of these, and thousands of other missing children, the world over.

About the claim that the PJ were recommended to precede on the assumption of death in the appartment.

**** said,

I don't think there can be too much doubt that Bennett has libelled them, *****. Over on the 3As, ****** has subjected John Lowe's emails from the files to forensic examination in respect of *PJ Officer Jaoa Carlos'* assertion that the forensic reports indicated Madeleine had died in the apartment. And ******'s assessment is that Carlos misinterpreted the e-mails.

More than that, from Amaral's book (and I can find the part if you want me to) Amaral went against the bet-

ter counsel of Martin Grimes and Mark Harrison in pro-
ceeding on an accusatory basis against the McCanns.

Yet Bennett has it that Mark Harrison recommended
that the whole investigation should proceed on the basis
that Madeleine died in the apartment.

And that's just to start.

About Mr Bennett's rather poor maths!

**** said,
   'That' publication 'suggests' that Madeleine's parents
went out and left the children 6 nights in a row. Considering they dined with the children in the Millennium restaurant for the first two nights 6 - 2 = 4. So they are going
to print with glaring mistakes and he has the cheek to try
and make other people take down what he calls libel and
inaccurate remarks!

**** said,
   Just looked this out, really this report is full of stuff
that the 'vanished' waiter said, like the wine which turned
out to be untrue, as only 2 bottles were on the docket for
the table!

**** said,
   *He said the group ate at the resort's other restaurant
on the first two nights of their holiday, a buffet restaurant called Millennium, and took all their children with
them.*

But they complained that the meal was too late for the youngsters and asked the Mark Warner manager to have the biggest table at the tapas bar, so they could leave their children in their nearby apartments while they ate.

The staff member's wife, who served the group at the Millennium, said the fractious children started crying towards the end of first two nights.

She said: "The children were generally very well-behaved, and I definitely remember Madeleine. She was like a little angel, very quiet and good as gold. Just a lovely little blonde girl.

"The second time they came in the McCanns were looking for the baby high chairs for their twins and Madeleine went over to the corner of the restaurant and started trying to drag them over.

"She obviously remembered where they were kept and wanted to help her parents, it was quite sweet really.

"Other than that she was just like any other little girl. She played with her food a little bit but didn't cause any trouble apart from that."

**** said,
I just wonder when the McCanns see a highly inaccurate mistake such as this, what they will do about it, for sure I do not think they are in any mood for ignoring it! We will see.

**** said,

Can't be sure but searching further, I believe the Mc-Canns arrived in Portugal on the 29th April & Madeleine went missing 3rd May that adds up to 5 days and nights there. They went to the Millennium restaurant on the 1st and 2nd nights so they were left in the apartment on 3 nights not 6 as he claims. I have never thought this man was very bright but I thought at least he could count, does not do a lot for his own credibility does he!

About the supposed concensus of opinion that Madeleine died in the appartment.

**** said,

So even if the dog alerted to blood that WAS Madeleine's, it could easily have come from the scrape we know she gave herself stumbling up the steps to the plane on the way out? Interesting.

**** said,

What makes me really angry, ****, is that two books peddle, actually, a number of myths: one in particular, that there was a consensus among the Portuguese contingent and the British contingent of the investigation team that Madeleine died in the apartment.

When you read Grimes' comments, you see that he does not hold, *period*, that dogs incriminate. He is very explicit and very plain. Dogs find evidence. In fact, not even that is true! *Keela* finds evidence. Eddie *indicates*. It's worth remembering that Keela is much the younger of the two dogs, and Eddie has spent a large proportion of his career working independently of her. Before Keela,

Eddie would have signalled and *human* eneavour (alone) would have looked for evidence of what Eddie had alerted to. Now Keela does that, much more efficently.

Grimes would say, simply, that *Keela* finds evidence where Eddie indicates; then it's the job of the boffins in the laboratries to examine the evidence Keela finds and determine questions of what tends to incriminate, or even, what exonerates. Grimes would have no truck with any suggestion that he was a part of a consensus view that Madeleine died in the apartment.

And when you read the (very long) report of Mark Harrison, the same is true. I guess Bennett could plead slipshod research as his excuse. Heaven only knows what excuse Amaral could plead.

**** said,
This has been bugging me a while and I've finally nailed it. From Bennett's text:

They [the PJ] turned for advice to experienced Leicestershire detective Mark Harrison, who, after a week's visit to Praia da Luz in July 2007 - in which he analysed all the evidence - advised that the Portuguese police should proceed on the working assumption that Madeleine had died in the McCanns' apartment,

Here is where the conclusion that Madeleine might have died in the apartment actually came from:

*The case file contains documents showing that Mark Harrison, the British search expert, and Martin Grimes, the dog-handler, **warned that the results should be treated with caution.** They insisted that "corroborating evidence" was* *needed and that no "intelligence reliability could be placed on the results".*

The Portuguese police, however, treated it very differently. On August 1, the day after the searches, <u>Inspector Joao Carlos</u>, one of the senior investigators, wrote to his superiors stating: "One must suppose that the child Madeleine McCann <u>could have died inside the apartment.</u>"

On the same day Carlos applied for court orders to bug the McCanns. The requests were rejected, but the police's intentions were clear. The McCanns noticed a distinct coldness which culminated in them being made suspects just over a month later.

About the apparent lack of evidence of an abductor.

**** said,

Have you heard about Mr Lino Henrique? I hadn't until I read the files more closely. But we all should have. I should make plain from the outset that Mr Henrique (I assume he's a man, though I'm not entirely certain) has no hidden secrets and is certainly not implicated in Madeleine's disappearance. But his part in the drama (in conjuction with other facts) goes a long way to nailing the pernicious canard of two books that underpins the traducement of at least 3 people (Gerry and Kate McCann and David Payne), possibly more: the canard, *all the evidence points to Madeleine having died in the apartment.* All the evidence actually points the other way. And the one-liner: *there is no evidence of an abductor* is a self-fulfiilng prophecy actually falls apart under close scrutiny. Unless you have the control DNA of the abductor, how can you know whether the abductor left any DNA evidence? You can't.

First a word about the operation of our intrepid canine duo, Eddie and Keela, in tandem. As has been pointed out (and is true!) Eddie always goes in first and Keela follows where Eddie indicates. Keela doesn't bother searching where Eddie doesn't indicate. From this (accurate) observation comes a fallacious assumption: that what Keela finds *must* be cadaverine, because Eddie has indicated such. It might be, or it might not, but forensic analysis *alone* determines the answer. Mr Henrique is very much alive.

So to apartment 5a. Control profiles were taken, not only of the McCanns (including Madeleine), but also of *all* visitors to the apartment after the McCanns vacated. One of those visitors was Mr Lino Henrique. Floor tiles and grouting between them, and other samples such as skirting board were taken up from areas where Keela indicated and were sent to Birmingham for analysis. The files carry a series of reports detailing the results of tests carried out. A profile matching of that of Mr Lino Henrique was produced -- as well as the profiles of two people (one male and one female) which did *not* match the control samples of anyone held. What if either of those was Madeleine's abductor?

Madeleine's name appears on only one report. As with the material recovered from the boot of the Renault, it was impossible to determine the nature of the sample from which the profile was established, and it wasn't positively identified as Madeleine's. The point should be emphasised that to find Madeleine's DNA would scarcely be surprising and certainly not, in and of itself, incriminating of her parents. She lived there the best part of a week. Of course her DNA was (and is) going to be in the apartment.

So there you have it, folks. The *truth* behind the lie of: *Maddie: The Truth Behind The Lie.*

**** said,
Wow, thanks for that ****.

This goes to show the importance of just not believing the dogs but believing and trusting the analysis of what the dogs find. To be able to match profiles enough to confirm who the DNA belongs to, the markers must have been 100% equal to that of Mr Henrique and the same said of the known visitors. More profound though, we have positivley identified Two unknown persons in 5A without a profile. Confirmed as they indicate a Male and a Female which do not match the profile of known visitors.

I wonder if this man and women have been considered by Goncalo? They should have been if he considered wishy washy evidence to make the McCanns arguido's. But I saw no mention of it and didn't know about it until you just brought it to my attention.

So more evidence to confirm a possible abduction. I hope the resulting DNA has been kept and stored for when a match is required.

**** said,
This is really good stuff, ****. Much of this I hadn't thought of before. I especially noticed the bit reading:

**** quote: **"Unless you have the control DNA of the abductor, how can you know whether the abductor left
any DNA evidence? You can't."**

That particularly rings true.

Abduction of a Child from Home - Further Information.

**** said,

I just watched 20/20 about the case of Riley Fox. She
was a beautiful three year old that disappeared while
asleep on the couch in the family home. She was later
found dead in the river. She had been raped, bound
with duct tape and thrown into the water alive, and had
drowned. This happened in Wilmington Illinois, just ou-
side of Chicago in 2004.

I wont go into the whole details of what happened
next, but many months later after a very lengthy interrogation (and with elections for DA etc within weeks) he
confessed to killing his daughter. His brother got a very
good defence attorney interested and she only takes cases where she believes the accused to be guilty. The police
made up some ridiculous theory about him accidentally
killing her, then staging it to look like a sexual assault
(doesnt quite explain why he threw his live daughter in
the river though). The defense was able to get DNA on
the Y chromosome from the child, which proved it wasnt
the father. So he was exonerated. He was facing the death
penalty.

As to why he confessed, it apparently has to do with a
14 hour interrogation and not being able to see a way out

of the room. It is apparently quite common, according to the defense attorney, which is why corroborating evidence is mandatory. But the DNA was hard to get, so the police decided they didn't need it (a very small sample). The defense pursued it and it proved he was innocent. The police also did other things, insisting no abduction took place because there was no evidence of break in (but the back door was broken and there ws evidence the person was looking for a way out), the blanket she was wrapped in wasnt tested, no fingerprinting done of the window (looking for a way out) or the door, and then it looks as thought the police got stuck in a rut and took the wrong path. Any of this sounding familiar?

Why am I telling this story?

Riley was abducted from her home and murdered, but by someone who is not of her family. It may be that the culprit is known to the family, or it may be that is a predatory paedophile who took a liking to the little girl, but whoever it was took a chance on stealing the girl out of the house while the father was home. The mother was away for the night.

Children are abducted from their homes by strangers, or acquaintances, or neighbourhood people. Not all crimes concerning children in their own homes are done by the parents.

Let me quote one of the Fox's defense witnesses, Professor Ann Burgess

Professor Ann Burgess of Boston College, who was worked with the FBI profiling killers, testified on behalf of the Foxes that cases involving intruders are not

as rare as many think. "There're many cases where an intruder comes in and and takes a child, Elizabeth Smart, absolutely perfect case."

If you would like to read more about this here is the link to the 20/20 story.

http://abcnews.go.com/TheLaw/Story?id=6196896&page=1

This is a portal to a site that has the video and transcript. About half way down the page is a reference to 'Who killed Riley Fox?"and links to the video.

And I want to add.

Prof Burgess is an EXPERT in this field. Mr Bennet is NOT. Which one will you believe?

**** said,
   ****, this case is an example of why no-one can be trusted with the death penalty.

Too many examples of police/judicial incompetence, corruption and the gullibility/blood-lust of the public.

No-way are we there yet .. so we just have to stomach the injustice of the obviously guilty not being sufficiently punished... to protect the innocents who are still being framed in too many countries .. 3rd world and 1st too.

And there is JonBenet .. her pyscopathic killer(s) is still out there... and her parents were almost framed for her slaughter & it has taken years to exonerate them too.

Their lives were ruined beyond repair and Patsy died never knowing who murdered her beautiful daughter.

**** said,

I just went to abc news and I watched the video, it is in several parts and you have to scroll down to pick the others up after watching the first part. One thing semed to jump out at me, the police say Kevin Fox confessed to killing Riley accidentally and then staged it to look like an abduction and that he placed duct tape ver her mouth and placed her in the river, if he killed her, why would he put tape over her mouth before putting her in the river?

I cannot believe how many eerie similarities there with Riley's abduction, to that of Madeleine McCann's. So much for bennett's book.

I suggest that BEFORE bennett goes much further with his ridiculous book, that he views the footage of what happened to Riley's daddy.

When is there going to be a public inquiry held into the dreadful bungling of the investigation of Madeleine McCann's abduction?

Bennett and his cohorts appear to be on some kind of power trip, they really believe they have the right to demand answers of the McCanns, they don't! If they really want to help children as they say they want to do, then they will add to the growing calls and pressure for Portugal to hold a full and independent public inquiry. Until this basic step is taken, no one, least of all Madeleine's parents are going to discover what happened to Madeleine.

God bless these poor children.

Until then one word sums up what I think and feel about bennett and his cohorts and that is - PATHETIC!

**** said,
The Foxes were very unlucky to have lost Riley that way, but very lucky that it didnt result in the loss of the father as well. It was only a very good defense attorney who questioned an 'inconclusive' finding on the DNA taken from Riley's body, that resulted in his acquittal.

The similarities really concern just what happens when a miscarriage of justice takes place. The sheriff etc clearly went on the wrong track about the father, and did from the start. Why else would they not have done forensics on the blanket, or treated the whole house as a crime scene, taking fingerprints from the doors and windows, and checking for things such as blood in the house.

I was so upset when I watched the show, especially about how little Riley died. So young, so beautiful, so innocent. But I made myself watch it because I knew that the DNA had been used to free the father, I saw the ad. And I could see the similarities between that and Madeleine's case. Also, I saw shorts of Prof Burgess, and this is exactly the thing that makes Bennett look to be a fool, so I forced myself to watch. Crying a lot about that beautiful little girl.

Yesterday was a bad day for me. I watched the 20/20 show about Riley, read the NOTW article about Baby P (Peter). Completely overwhelming. I wish I hadnt read about Baby P, but I am glad I watched the show about

Riley. Perhaps this information will help the McCanns. And after this, my kids got lots of cuddles and hugs.

One thing as well. This re-inforces my point about a lone predatory paedophile. I have always felt if it was a lone paedophile, that Madeleine's body would have been found, as they dont cover their tracks very well. As with Riley. She was dumped and left to drown, only a few km's from her home. And this is because it is too risky to go far with the body in the car. This person will have killed before and will kill again.

The thing is ****, about the police theory, is that the father would not have taped her mouth and thrown her in the river alive, albeit unconcious (as the theory goes). If he thought she was dead, he would have called 911. But even if he wanted to try to remove the evidence,he wouldnt have mutilated his daughter and tied her up. And remember the police theory is that he accidentally killed her (or thought he did) by knocking her into the wall or the bath or something. It is just as stupid as cutting up Joanne and feeding her to the pigs, or placing Madeleine in the freezer. Thank goodness for the tiny DNA sample, which although cannot be used to show who killed her, can definitely be used to exclude people.

**** said,
Isn't Carlos Rodriguez, the private detective in Riley's case, the same private detective that went to Portugal and talked to everyone undercover? **He concluded that Madeleine had been abducted.**

Apparently he is part Portuguese, so could converse with people fluently about that night.

About what Mr bennett said about the strenght of the dog evidence.

**** said,

I think Mr. Bennett has been oversold the Dog evidence just like the PJ were.

Mr. Bennett Quotes:-

"According to the official police summary report released in July this year - and confirmed by video evidence of the dogs in action in Praia da Luz, widely available on the Internet - Eddie, the cadaver dog, found the 'smell of death' in the following places. We quote the exact words of the report"

For full details of Bennetts report, please see point no. 2 on the thread. I just wanted to highlight in this post he makes no mention of the cautionary advice given by Mr. Grimes, which was

NO EVIDENTIAL OR INTELLIGENCE RELIABILITY CAN BE MADE FROM THIS ALERT UNLESS IT CAN BE CONFIRMED WITH CORROBERATING EVIDENCE.

Rather important words to miss out wouldnt you say!

So Mr. Bennett, in your conclusion, you tell us we should note 3 important things, could I suggest you change that to 4 by including the words of Mr. Grimes, The Dog Handler, after all we dont want to be mislead do we!

You also say, "in addition Mr Harrison and Mr Grimes, who trained Eddie and Keela, patiently explained that the dogs had traced the 'smell of death' - human cadaverine - on around 200 previous occasions. They had never once been wrong".

I would say, to know they had never been wrong, then there must have been either a body or corroberating evidence or that statement could never be made.

I would also like to add the opinion of a former Scotland Yard dog handler:-

John Barrett, a former Scotland Yard dog handler, also indicated that the trained dogs used in an attempt to detect a "death smell" on Mrs McCann's Bible and clothes were brought in too long after Madeleine vanished.

The crucial scent lasts for no longer than a month, he said.

**** said,
Mr Bennett quotes:-

(d) Fourth, the Doctors McCann claimed that the 'smell of death' could have come from rotting meat that Gerry McCann was taking to the local rubbish dump from time to time. This is also impossible, as the scent from dead animals does not produce the same 'cadaverine' as human cadaver scent. The cadaver dogs are trained to detect only human cadaverine. Probably Dr Gerry McCann didnt realise this when he made his coment.

Now read these excerpts and see how many times the word PIG comes up:-

Source The Independant 28.05.08.

A trained human cadaver dog will not signal a living person or an animal (except PIGS), but it will signal a recently deceased, putrefying or skeletonised human corpse. That suggests that the "bouquet of death" is discernible, but attempts to identify it have so far failed. Two of the by-products of decomposition, putrescine and cadaverine, have been bottled and are commercially available as dog training aids. But they are also present in all decaying organic material, and in human saliva.

A human cadaver dog's detection skills depend greatly on its training, and the problem is that human remains are hard to come by. Trainers often use a combination of available "pseudoscents", and PIGS. The problem with pseudoscents, says Mick Swindells, a retired police handler who works as a freelance trainer and handler in Blackpool, is that they represent a "snapshot" of death. As decomposition proceeds, the chemistry of the corpse evolves, causing its odour to change. "I'm trying to train a dog to find the whole video, not just a snapshot," he says. PIGS decompose in similarly to humans, and when buried they disturb the ground in a similar way.

Swindells says: "The best thing about using a dog to detect cadavers, as opposed to machines, is that dogs have the ability to think. But that's also the worst thing about using dogs." This means that cadaver dogs appear to have sufficient intelligence to recognise a corpse across a range of environmental conditions. However, they can also be distracted, for example by methane produced naturally in a peat bog (corpses also produce methane).

Source BBC News Site 26.09.06.

The dogs on the team range from small terriers to spaniels and mongrels and are trained for the cadaver work using PIGS, as pork is "80 - 85% as near to human flesh as you can get without the real thing", he said.

Source Search & Rescue dogs Forum.

The scent from a PIG can produce the same cadavarine as a human. There is no detectable difference between rotting PIG and human (apparently after a time the scents are the same). They train with PIG bone, flesh and human bone.

The above are particular excerpts lifted from articles I have read. I do not decry the work of these dogs, these excerpts are just to show what Bennett is saying as fact is not so!

Nobody knows how Eddie was trained as according to the BBC article "Sniffing through the concrete" The specialist training techniques - which are highly confidential - were developed by Eddie's handler Martin Grimes, along with the UK's National Policing Improvement Agency (NPIA) and America's Federal Bureau of Investigation (FBI).

They are scientifically based and rely on how dogs smell and the chemicals involved.

On the subject of Jane Tanner's account of the abductor.

**** said,

You really have to question the credibility of Bennett's research. Well thankfully that is what we are doing, here he refers to JT's first statement:

"Jane Tanner's first description of the abductor she claimed to have seen was that he had short hair, was of average height and build, and 'was carrying a bundle, maybe a blanket'. She also claimed that she had seen the abductor on her way back from visiting her apartment to check on the children, and said that the abductor was working in a northerly direction, i.e. away from the beach"

Now read her actual first statement given 04.05.07 at 11:30am

Jane Tanner's description of the individual:

(*) Brown male between 35 and 40, slim, around 1.70m. Very dark hair, thick, long at the neck. (Noticed when the person was seen from the back). He was wearing golden beige cloth trousers (linen type) with a "Duffy" type coat (but not very thick). He was wearing black shoes, of a conventional style and was walking quickly. He was carrying a sleeping child in his arms across his chest. By his manner, the man gave her the impression that he wasn't a tourist.

(**) Concerning the child, who seemed to be asleep, she only saw the legs. The child seemed to be bigger than a baby. It had no shoes on, was dressed in cotton light-coloured pyjamas (perhaps pink or white) It is uncertain, but the interviewee has the feeling that she saw a design on the pyjamas like flowers, but is not certain about it.

Concerning these details, the interviewee states not having known what Madeleine was wearing when she disappeared. She has not spoken to anyone about this. Concerning the man, she has only mentioned it to Gerald, but without going into details and with the police. The interviewee has been invited to draw a sketch which we attach to this document. Questioned, she stated probably being able to identify the person that she saw if she saw him in profile and at the place where she saw him.

After reading, goes on and signs.

Mr. Bennett then refers to her 2nd statement:-

"Then, when she gave a second statement days later - and of course after she had had time to confer with the Doctors McCann - she changed her story and told the Portuguese police that she distinctly remembered seeing a blonde-haired girl wearing pyjamas 'with a pinkish aspect'. Once again, there is no rational explanation as to why she did not 'remember' these details when first questioned".

Now read JT 2nd Statement 10.05.07. Only a very rough translation, but you should get the drift.

What really happened to your front, a man carrying at the neck, a barefoot child. At the time, it gave due attention because it is normal in the Ocean Club, children spend the lap of parents from the nursery to the their homes, when they will get to the babby-sitting service. Only surprised that the child does not get any coverage (blanket) and how individuals walking, so hurried, as wearing the trousers were slightly wide throughout its length, being right.

They were, in color, similar to "corticite," type "Chinese" (sic.). As for the jacket was dark, unable to specify the same, which seemed to be of the same material of the pants, is a type "anorak" (sic.). As for footwear states that can not rely with complete sure, but shoes with a slight"tacãoV. v

---

About description of the child, confided that it was transported to the pass, with the legs in his direction and barefoot. He thought it was a female child because the pajamas was light-colored (pink seemed to him). I never saw the child's hair. I never saw her move to ned any sound, thinking he was sleeping.

If Bennett is going to discredit the main witness to suit his own agenda, he should at least get his facts straight. Its disgraceful what he is doing and I hope the McCanns and all the other people he is insinuating are liars sue his backside off.

On the failure of the friends to take part in the search for Madeleine.

The startling failure of the McCanns' friends to search for Madeleine the night she disappeared.

According to a number of reports which have never been contradicted, while hundreds of people, including staff of Mark Warners and many local people, searched the area around the Ocean Club apartments for hours after Madeleine went missing, not one of the McCanns' friends, known as the 'Tapas 9?, bothered to do so. They all went to bed. That was confirmed in articles written by Bridget O'Donnell (Jeremy Wilkins' partner) of The Guardian and David James Smith of The Times in December 2007. That is as clear an indication as you could get that they knew it would be pointless searching for Madeleine. It is entirely consistent with them knowing that Madeleine was already dead.

**** said,

Oh really Mr Bennett? If you say they have never been contradicted I would suggest you do a little more research, this took me seconds to contradict you!

What do you have to say about this?

'Help me, please help me'. She said, 'We've been searching all night until 4.30am, and then everybody left us'. At that stage there was only one police officer at the door. They didn't know what to do.

There is also reports of other people that saw and HEARD Gerry McCann wandering around crying out his daughter's name in the early hours of the morning!

Is Bennett in denial, or is he suffering from some kind of selective amnesia?

Is this really the quality of the research of a supposed learned professional? This is a bloody disgrace what is happening here and he and his book needs to be stopped!

"The McCanns were immediately certain that their daughter had been kidnapped and determined to publicise her disappearance as widely as possible, ensuring that, from the very first moments, the hunt for Madeleine was as much about the media coverage as it was the police investigation. Jill Renwick has known the couple since they all worked together at a Glasgow hospital more than a decade ago. She spoke to Kate at 7am on the morning after Madeleine vanished: "She just said, *'Help me, please help me'. She said, 'We've been searching all night until 4.30am, and then everybody left us'. At that stage there was only one police officer at the door. They didn't know what to do.* So I phoned GMTV."

She also phoned the McCanns' wider circle of friends, who mobilized to phone anyone they could think of to beg for help. Renwick's sister called someone she knew in CID, someone had a connection with Des Browne, the defence secretary. One friend lives close to the Newsnight presenter Kirsty Wark, said Renwick: "She knocked on her door and said, 'I know you must think I'm mad but my friend's wee girl is missing, can you do anything to help?' Though they are not friends, Gordon Brown's brother John lives in the same street as Renwick: *"I stopped him in the street the day afterwards and said, 'These are my friends. Do you think you could speak to Gordon about it?' And he said of course.* I don't know if anything came about that way."

**** said,

If Mr. Bennett is going to quote media sources as fact, David James Smith of the Times December 17th also stated:-

"The PJ had never attempted to obtain a "control sample" of Madeleine's DNA. That had been left to the McCanns, who had found traces of her saliva on the pillow of her bed at home in Rothley and provided that DNA sample to the Portuguese police".

I say, this is not exactly the actions of guilty parents who knew their daughter was already dead is it ?

**** said,

Seeing as Mr. Bennett has singled 2 particular articles out as confirmation that the friends failed to search, I have located the 2 articles I believe he is referring to and I would invite you to read them as I can see "no clear indication" as Mr. Bennett puts it, to confirm that the Tapas believed searching for Madeleine was pointless.

David Smith James:-

http://www.timesonline.co.uk/tol/news/world/europe/article3040094.ece

Bridget O'Donnell

http://www.guardian.co.uk/crime/article/0,,2227416,00.html

So there we have it. Just some of the many examples we have found of sloppy or totally absent research, misquoted statements and complete falseifications within Mr Bennett's book. We say it should now, with immediate effect, be banned from sale to the public, as it contravenes trading standards as being proven to be factually incorrect, and in many cases, potentially libelous.

18. A summary of Mr Bennett's reasons: Plus some facts he would have you ignore.

1. 'Stranger' abductions of an infant from a family home almost never happen. We always need to examine whether the family may be involved.

(Mr Bennett claims the highly dubious figure of 99% of all claimed abductions were actually staged by the parents as some form of cover up. So far we have been unable to find Mr. Bennett's source. The only figure we can find, from Britain's Psychological Offender Profiling Committee for the Home Office, is considerably lower, somewhat less than 70%. If we used Mr Bennett's flawed reasoning as a basis for conviction, then over 30% of all parents of missing children would by now be in jail for crimes they didn't commit. Think about that for a moment. It should also be pointed out that we have listed over twenty cases elswhere of children who HAVE been abducted by strangers, many of whom are still missing.)

2. The evidence from two highly trained cadaver dogs that the 'smell of death' was found in several places in the holiday apartment where the McCanns were staying - and in a car they hired three weeks later.

(Eddie and Keela, the two sniffer dogs, are both English Springer Spaniels. However, Mr Bennett bizarrly claims that one of the sniffer dogs is in fact a bloodhound, a species almost twice as large as the Spaniel. We can only assume he did not, at any time, watch the video's of the dogs in action. What then, we wonder, qualifies him to pass any judgement on what the dogs indicated? We would also like to remind you of the report of the dog's handler, Martin Grimes, who makes it quite clear that without coroberating forensic evidence, the dogs indications are worthless, and that in his opinion the indications were possibly as the result of cross-contamination.)

3. The extraordinary reactions of Doctors Kate and Gerry McCann when they were told that the cadaver dog and the bloodhound had detected the 'smell of death' and blood in Apartment 5a and the Renault Scenic.

(The PJ presented this as 'Evidence' to the McCann's, and were insistant that it proved Madeleine was dead, despite warnings from Mr Grimes that without coroboration, these dog indications meant nothing. In the face of such a dogmatic attitude, it is no wonder the McCann's were desperate to think of any other possibility, knowing themselves to be innocent.)

4. The forensic evidence of the DNA of blood found in the living room of the McCanns' apartment, and in the Renault Scenic hired by the McCanns, analysed by the Forensic Science Service here in England.

(DNA evidence which, as we now know, was inconclusive, and should not have formed part of any investigation. It should also be noted that as of this moment, TWO sets of DNA have yet to be identified, wether staff or guests. How can it possibly be ruled out that one or both of these sets could be from the abductors?)

5. Dr Kate McCann's refusal to answer any of the questions put to her by the Portuguese police - especially Question No. 41.

(Kate was advised by her solicitor NOT to answer these questions, so this does not qualify for use as a 'reason.' Further, if you had an experienced, professional solicitor present, there to protect your best interests, would you take her advice, or ignore it?)

6. Publicly agreeing to take a lie detector test - and then refusing.

(Kate was very keen to take a lie detector test, but on two provisions. Firstly that she could be sure it was 100% accurate, and secondly that it would be admisible as evidence in court. Unfortunatly no such guarantee could be made for the accuracy, and she was told that lie detector results were, in fact, inadmissable as evidence. So she therefore decided it simply wasn't worth it after all.)

7. The sheer impossibility of the abduction happening as claimed.

(See our chapter, The Sheer Imposibility.)

8. The McCanns' immediate and insistent cry of 'abduction' - excluding all other possibilities.

(For us on the outside, there are three possibilities: Accidental or deliberate homicide, she wandered off, or abduction. Kate, however, knowing full well she did not kill Madeleine would only have a choice of two. Since she above all others would know Madeleine's likely reactions on waking up alone, (She is known to get into her parent's bed, even if it's empty.) and given the fact, verified by the first GNR reports, that the window was open, her ONLY logical assumption was abduction. There simply are no other possibilities.)

9. The McCanns' false claim that the abductor had forced entry by jemmying open the shutters.

(In their panic, a logical assumption. The window WAS open when the first GNR arrived, as backed up in their initial reports.)

10. The shutters could only be opened from the inside - and only Kate McCann's fingerprints were on the window.

(Most likely scenario? Two abductors, one inside, one outside. First abductor, wearing gloves, enters through unlocked door, opens window, quickly passes Madeleine to accomplace to facilitate speedy withdrawal and minimise the chances of any cries being heard at the front of the building. They then split up and make their escape.)

11. Contradictions between the account of Jeremy Wilkins and the accounts of Dr Gerry McCann and Jane Tanner.

(Any policeman will tell you witness accounts always vary. If they are a perfect match then the police instantly suspect foul play, as there is evidence of a pre-planned and rehersed story)

12. The failure of both the Doctors McCann, and their friend Jane Tanner, to talk to each other for 24 hours about her claimed sighting of the alleged abductor.

(Odd, don't you think, that Mr Bennett is accusing the whole group of getting together to plan some sort of cover up, then saying they DIDN'T get together to discuss what would be the most important part of this cover up? Which is it, Mr Bennett? What is most likely is that the parents were far to busy talking to police, to other witnesses or the press.)

13. The insistence of Gerry McCann in releasing a description of the abductor based solely on the claims about an alleged abductor made by Jane Tanner - and with the reluctant consent of the Portuguese police.

(This is STANDARD PROCEDURE in this country. If you have a suspect, for any crime, you give out a description. Police reticence was purely down to fear of affecting the local tourist trade.)

14. Ignoring advice not to highlight Madeleine's 'coloboma' eye defect.

(The EXPERT advice was the EXACT OPPOSITE to that from the PJ. The American 'National Centre for Missing and Exploited Children,' plus our own Child Rescue

Alert system advise getting the child's face in the public eye as soon as possible.)

15. Making long-term plans to mark Madeleine's alleged abduction - whilst at the same time claiming she was alive and could still be found.

(It's called hoping for the best, while planning for the worst.)

16. Jane Tanner's ever-changing stories of what the alleged abductor looked like - and other problems with Jane Tanner's accounts.

(On the contrary, though press acounts may have varied about what Jane Tanner has said, her accounts, as given to, and recorded in, the official police files, match perfectly.)

17. Gerry McCann's absolute insistence that the abductor was the man allegedly seen by Jane Tanner.

(Jane Tanner described a man carrying a child wearing the same pjamas as Madeleine. What assumption would YOU have made?)

18. The commitment of the McCanns and their 'Tapas 9? friends to a 'Pact of Silence' about what had happened to Madeleine.

(The word used in the Portuguese press when correctly translated, means 'Agreement,' not 'pact.' What was actually said was that they had an agreement not to talk to the press, in order to comply with the strict secrecy laws.)

19. The startling failure of the McCanns' friends to search for Madeleine the night she disappeared.

(TOTALLY wrong. MANY eye witness acounts contradict this. SEVERAL of the friends, AND Gerry were seen out that night looking for Madeleine, and heard calling her name.)

20. Frequent changes to their story and numerous contradictions.

(As stated before, in any police examination of witnesses, a certain amount of differences and contradictions are expected. Also as time passes other details are remembered and added to later statements.)

21. The hiring of very dubious firms of so-called 'private investigators.'

(They percieved the PJ as failing them, what else would any concerned parents do? The group were recommended to them. The REAL question is, if they DID have something to hide, what was the purpose of hiring a detective agency at all?)

22. The McCanns' rush, right from the outset, to hire a team of top lawyers, including the appointment of Britain's top extradition lawyer.

(These lawyers all came to the McCann's, and offered their services. The McCann's did not 'Rush' to aproach anyone.)

23. Not staying protectively close to the twins after Madeleine's disappearance.

(They could have stayed at home, by the phone, wringing their hands in desperation, or they could take a proactive aproach, taking a firm lead and personally getting involved with the search for their daughter. What would YOU do?)

24. The McCanns' apprehension about their 'phone calls and e-mails being monitored'

(No evidence is given by Mr Bennett to back up this claim. How does he know what they were worried about?)

25. Kate McCann's decision to wash 'Cuddle Cat' - the pink toy - despite the McCanns' belief that it may have been handled by the abductor.

(Kate did not, in fact, wash CuddleCat untill THREE MONTHS after the abduction. It was the PJ who failed to do proper forensic tests on Madeleine's favourite toy on day one. Kate can hardly be blamed for the PJ incompetence in this case.)

26. Failing to co-operate fully with the Portuguese police despite repeatedly promising to do so - and refusing their mobile 'phone records.

(Wrong. The McCann's did NOT in fact refuse their phone records. The PJ issued a request to obtain the full details of the records to the chief prosecutor. HE turned them down, on the grounds that it violated their right to privacy. In addition, the list of the TIMES of phone calls from both before AND after the abduction are listed in the official report. If the McCann's HAD refused, how did the records get into the files?)

27. Having a ready supply of pre-printed photographs of Madeleine ready for the police as soon as they arrived on the night of 3rd May.

(Obviously, the first thing the police would ask for, when dealing with a missing child, is recient photographs. This is the account of Amy Tierney, from the official PJ files.

When questioned and shown the photographs referred to in the previous statements, depicting the English girl, on "Kodak Xtra Life " paper, 10 x 15, she said they were printed on her printer, also of Kodak brand. When on the night of 3rd May, at about 24.00, she was at her desk at the Tapas bar, inside the resort, when at a certain time, one of the friends of the McCann couple, Russell, asked for a USB memory stick reader, in order to print photographs of Madeleine. Immediately the deponent replied that she did not have an USB reader, but that she had a printer with this hardware, which could read from memory sticks.

She went to her room and returned to the Tapas with the printer where **she printed out 20 to 30 photographs** of the girl, using her own paper, in **10x15** format mentioned previously. The memory stick containing the photos belonged to the McCann couple, and came from their camera.

She thinks that all of this took place at about 24.00 on 3rd May 2007. She presumes that she handed all of the photos to Russell, who distributed some to those present, the rest would be for the police authorities.)

28. Not releasing the famous 'last photo' of Madeleine, taken at the poolside, for three weeks - and only after Gerry had returned to England.

(The first priority was to release good, clear images of Madeleine, those that would be of the most help in identifying her, and in particular her distinctive eye mark, to the public. It was the press who were hungry for more, previously unseen pictures, and it was for this reason the 'Last' picture was released.)

29. The strange words and phrases the McCanns have used in referring to the alleged abduction.

(Such as 'It's a disaster?' If one of your children were abducted, would you not consider it a disaster?)

30. Only carrying out a drugs test on the twins after five months.

(An attempt to claim Kate was deliberatly stalling, till it would be too late to prove anything. However, drug residue stays in the hair for a very long time. Tests carried out on Shannon Mathews showed that she had been repeatedly drugged for over TWENTY months. Furthermore, these tests were in fact carried out to prove that Kate HADN'T drugged the children, and silence the critics, rather than that the abductor HAD.)

Finally, though we cannot be sure, not having wasted our money on a copy of Mr Bennett's leaflet, we can make a safe assumption that the following three points will raise their heads at some point in the second half of his booklet, all based on internet speculation and press fraud.

Point one involves the marking of Kate's Bible at a passage supposedly involving the death of a child. We are sure Mr Bennett's flawed reasoning would lead him to suppose this is another reason to suspect abduction. However, refering back to the official PJ files, we find this statement, from **the original owner** of the Bible, who lent it to Kate to give her some comfort. No doubt Mr Bennett would far rather his readers did not know of the following statement.

"I have a tendency to mark pages and passages in the bible and even though this was my spouse's bible, there were many marked/tagged passages relevant to the both of us. This happened before Madeleine's disappearance.

I encouraged Kate to read Psalms X and XX of the Old Testament as I felt these were relevant to her. They are both believers. The Psalms reveal a confidence in God, in his justice and in the question which can be asked "Why do bad things happen". Psalms XX is a small oration asking Him to guide and illuminate our path in times of anguish.

The passage which is marked in my wife's bible I believe is Samuel 2:12. This passage is very significant for me and my wife but likely has so significance for Kate. I interpret this passage as saying that even though we cannot be with the two children that we have now lost, we will find them one day.

After meeting with Kate, I returned to Lagos and caught a taxi to Portimao where I had previously (May 2003) visited a Christian bookstore. I went with the purpose to acquire a new bible to help me through the rest of the week. Unfortunately, I did not find the bookstore.

The second point is the release of so-called 'Extracts from Kate's diary.' In these supposed extracts, Kate allegedly wrote, BEFORE Madeleine's abduction, about how Madeleine was hyper-active, was difficult to control, and was wearing her down. She supposedly commented in a negative way about Gerry's supposed lack of help with the children, and how he was always off playing tennis, instead of helping Kate. And she supposedly mentioned the medication she was on, to control her anxiety attacks. This story is still passed around the internet as fact. IT IS NOT! These 'Extracts' were the work of a Portuguese journalist, faked on the orders of his editor, in order to sell more copies. This revelation was made by a rather shamefaced PJ official in a rare televised press interview, who admitted that this story was indeed not true, and that the PJ were considering charging this journalist with wasting the PJ's time. Kate did not, in fact, start keeping a diary until several weeks AFTER Madeleine was abducted, on the suggestion of one of her aunt's, as a way of keeping a record of the efforts everyone in the family had made to find Madeleine. When she is eventually found, Madeleine would then be able to read for herself how her mother and father never once gave up hope of finding her."

The third point is the McCann's supposed refusal to take part in a reconstruction of the events of the night Madeleine was taken. This point needs to be cleared more than any other, as it is still one of the biggest sticks the critics on the less intellectual forums use to beat the parents with. Firstly, a short time after the abduction, the parents practically BEGGED the PJ to do a televised 'Crimewatch' style reconstruction, hoping this would yield vital evidence as to Madeleine's whereabouts. THE PJ REFUSED TO ALLOW THIS. Their reasons for refusal have never been given. Then, almost a year later, the PJ REQUESTED the McCann's and their friends to return to Portugal to take part in a reconstruction. Note, they were REQUESTED, not ordered as many think, to return. Again the parents asked that it be televised, and also there were worries about whether any of the friends would face arrest on arrival. The PJ AGAIN refused to allow the reconstruction to be televised, this time explaining it was just for their own records, nothing more. The parents explained that they were only interested in anything that could help find Madeleine. A reconstruction that no one would ever see, sitting instead gathering dust in some police storage facility is NOT going to help find anyone, and since the PJ were also evasive about guaranteeing the fact about if the friends would end up in jail or not, the McCann's wisely declined the invitation. To the authors, all of this had only one purpose. To further blacken the name of the McCann's in the public eye, by putting them in a 'no-win' situation. But we are sure Mr Bennett will not give the full story behind these points, just as he has been economical with the truth behind his other reasons. This is why we need to make the FULL facts be known, so you, the reader, can decide for yourself, who is telling the truth.

19. A FINAL WORD TO TONY BENNETT.

How many other parents would you charge with neglect?

How many times have we heard the line, "If they hadn't have left the kids alone, it would never have happened?" It is the be all and end all for many of the McCann's sterner critics, as if that somehow ends the discussion right there and then. That comment is often followed by "We go on holiday as a family, and stay together as a family." "They dumped the kids in the crèche all day while they went off and enjoyed themselves." We must presume that these people's children, given a choice, would rather stay close to the old crusties than join one of the myriad of kids clubs that almost every family resort offers. From our experience, when on holiday in similar resorts, it is not so much a case of 'Dumping' the kids in these crèches/clubs, but trying to stop them from joining in the fun with the other kids! And what, prey tell, could be wrong with that?

The fact is, even now, at the time of going to print, this particular author still has the ability to be stunned by the level and degree of venom their story continues to excite among a, thankfully, small minority of the general public.*

The want of compassion among these few is shocking; the desire to punish the parents shaming. This is not to say that any of the authors of this book agrees with what the parents did. The McCanns did leave their three children unattended for half an hour at a time while they and their friends had dinner. Their behaviour carried risks for the children, one of the worst of which was realised. But we all agree their actions were based on naivety, a holiday induced feel-good factor, not criminal neglect.

We also agree that the price this couple has paid, and continue to pay to this day, is beyond anything we ourselves could possibly imagine. The suffering they have endured negates any necessity for reprimand. Does even their sternest judge imagine they are not their own greatest critics; that they aren't consumed by regret and remorse?

We, the authors, and other members of our forum have been highly critical of the Portuguese police, and their investigation into Madeleine's abduction. Indeed Portugal's attorney-general made a statement in which he said the McCanns were named as suspects in the absence of any evidence. According to our favoured few, however, our real motivation is to support middle-class doctors against working-class police officers. The McCanns put their pleasure before their children, they say. If they were working class, and lived on a housing estate, the British police would have been waiting for them on the tarmac and falling over themselves to prosecute. The McCanns should be prosecuted for neglect, is their battle cry. These people don't even mention the abductor.

You might have thought the fact that Kate and Gerry McCann are doctors would stand them in some regard, since they spend their lives trying to help others. Sadly, you would be wrong. We ourselves thought the clear evidence from family photographs that Madeleine was a happy, well-cared-for child would demonstrate that leaving her unsupervised was out of the ordinary, rather than the norm. But that position does not allow for jealousy and resentment.

So who else would you see charged with neglect Mr Bennett? If the McCanns are to stand in the dock, who should stand beside them? We can start with their friends, the so-called 'Tapas 7' all of whom were part of the routine of regular checkups, and any one of which could have been the unfortunate target of the abductor that night. Then what about all the other couples who have stayed at that or any family-friendly holiday village where they felt safe enough to leave the children unattended while they ate? What about all those families over the years who have stayed at Butlins, and left their children to the mercy of a radio equipped chalet maid? (Baby crying, chalet 221!) What about people who eat in the garden on hot summer evenings while their children sleep in the house? What about parents who sleep indoors, maybe one night a year, while their kids sleep in a tent?

There are some parents who pride themselves on their devotion but who would send their youngest to the park in the charge of their 12-year-old. There are many others who let their eight-year-old get the bus home from school. We the authors would not think of doing such things personally, but I'm sure there are some things that we have done that those parents, perhaps even among ourselves, that might be regarded as wrong.

When we leave the maternity ward of our local hospital, there is no nurse, no midwife handing out the manual on how to bring up our newborn child. We have to learn, from the school of life, by our mistakes, for we all make mistakes. Sometimes we can be too strict, other times too lax. We push them too hard, or take too little interest. We get grumpy and irritable if we don't get enough rest. Then we walk into their bedrooms when they're asleep, looking so small and so innocent, and we feel so bad inside for our failures of the day that we determine to do better tomorrow. We learn to deal with our mistakes because we also know, without doubt, that we love our children.

So tell us this, Mr Bennett. Do we want to see the courts filled with caring parents who made a mistake? Court is for the truly negligent and downright abusive. Parents, and we use that term loosely, like those of baby 'P' who died of the most horrific injuries. Mr Bennett set up his 'Madeleine foundation, (http://madeleinefoundation.org/main/) as a sort of personal platform from which to champion the rights of all neglected and abused children. But where on the Madeleine Foundation website is the case of baby 'P'? Where is the condemnation of Haringey council, who failed so completely to protect him? Where, in fact, is there any reporting whatsoever of all the dreadful and heart wrenching stories of child neglect, abuse and cruel murder that we have seen for ourselves in the press recently? We looked, long and hard, and the only child mentioned anywhere is Madeleine McCann.

How can Mr Bennett honestly expect anyone to take him seriously as the defender of all neglected and abused children, when his foundation has mention of only one little girl, a child who's parents clearly never caused her a single days neglect or abuse in her life?

The McCann's made a dreadful mistake, and are guilty of a terrible lapse of judgement. They did something stupid. But God forbid the government of this country ever made doing something stupid a crime. If they did, then the whole of the Isle of Wight would need to be turned into one vast open air prison, because each and every one of us would be guilty as charged.

Yes, Mr Bennett, even you.

*(A little word about our minority, and their tactic of 'Spamming.' Because there are so few of them, they have to try to puff themselves up, so as to appear bigger than they are. This is something oft seen in the animal kingdom, when a skunk, for instance, rears up on it's front legs, with hind quarters and tail arched menacingly over it's body, to appear larger and more intimidating to anything it supposes is a threat. This is what the members of certain hate forums do. At any time an article appears on a newspaper or news related website to do with the McCann's, and especially if the website has a comments facility, the word will spread on the forums, and a link to the article will appear. All the members then see it as their duty to 'Spam' or leave hateful and vitriolic comments in large numbers, leaving any genuine reader with the impression that the McCann's must be the most hated couple in the country. Such is the venom for this couple, that these hate sites seek to stifle any and all perceived

support for the McCann's. As we have said, a small minority, but a twisted one.)

20. CONCLUSION.

As we have now shown you, the nation of Portugal was, until comparatively recently, a dictatorship. Although great strides towards a true democracy have been made, the kind of freedoms, rights and justice system we in Great Britain take for granted are still not fully within the grasp of the average Portuguese citizen. We have corresponded with numerous Portuguese nationals, all of whom tell us stories of common people going into police stations only to emerge, sometimes days later, limping, or with bruises not evident when they first entered. Police brutality is still far too commonplace, with beatings being the norm, rather than the exception. Old habits, it seems, die hard. Amnesty International has expressed serious concerns to the European Parliament on a number of occasions, and the case of Leonor Cipriano, as documented elsewhere in this book, is at the time of writing soon to be heard at the European Court of Human Rights.

We have shown you several cases of child abduction and murder, and demonstrated the authorities' reactions, ranging from callous indifference to brutal aggression.

But we are not naive. We know we alone cannot change things overnight. But we can, perhaps, make a difference to one child, one family. And by doing so we hope that a chain reaction will be started, that a ball will start rolling, and we pray that other families will, in time, also benefit from our actions.

We demand that the Portuguese government implement a full and open public enquiry into the handling of the Madeleine McCann case, and fully investigate the actions and motives of the original police chief in charge, Goncalo Amaral. To this end, we have provided you, the reader, with a tear off page ready printed with our demands, for you to simply pop in the post to

The Foreign Secretary,
Foreign and Commonwealth Office,
King Charles Street,
London,
SW1A 2AH.

It will cost you just one postage stamp.

Portugal is a beautiful country. Its people have an unrivalled reputation for their warmth and hospitality. This generosity and welcoming attitude has meant that Portugal has long been a popular destination for thousands of families of tourists and holidaymakers from Britain and Europe. Every summer the resorts of areas like the Algarve are fully booked, the beaches crowded. But, through no fault of its people, Portugal has a problem, hanging over it like a dark and ominous shadow. Until the Portuguese authorities decide to open their eyes, and take action to remedy this situation, then Portugal cannot be considered a safe place to take children on holiday.

We wonder, in fact, is it safe for children at all?

To the Honourable Foreign Secretary,

Please forgive me for writing to you like this, but I have to share with you my gravest concerns about what I see as a grievous miscarriage of justice. I am talking about Kate and Gerry McCann, the long suffering parents of kidnapped Madeleine. Since purchasing and reading the book, 'The Madeleine Investigation: Incompetence or corruption' it has become ever more clear to me that the case was badly handled, indeed botched and bungled, to use the head of Scotland Yard's own words, since day one. I understand, of course, that Madeleine's abduction took place in Portugal, and was therefore not under British jurisdiction, but Madeleine, and of course her parents, Kate and Gerry, ARE British citizens, and have suffered greatly as a result of the gross miss-management of the case by the Portuguese authorities.

I have many questions I would like an answer to. For instance, why was the case originally handed to a police chief who was already at the time under investigation for the torture of the mother of another missing girl, Joanna Ciprianno? Such a thing would never happen in this country.

Who was the mysterious 'source close to the investigation' who leaked so many lies and rumours to the press? Mr and Mrs McCann were constantly threatened with two years in jail if they so much as breathed one word about the investigation, but this source seems to have flouted the so-called strict secrecy laws on an almost daily basis with impunity. Why has no attempt been made to discover this source, and bring them to justice?

Why were the results from the British FSS of the DNA evidence taken from Mr and Mrs McCann's hire car ignored by the police? The FSS said the results were inconclusive, and should in no way play any part of the investigation. But three days after they received these results the Portuguese police lied to Mr McCann, and told him the blood samples taken from their hire car were 100% positively Madeleine's. I find this fact in particular totally and wholly unacceptable.

I also have grave concerns regarding the use of the British sniffer dogs. Having watched the full length video of the use of these dogs, it is apparent that the dogs and their handler were manipulated into giving a false result. This false indication was, according to the police reports, instrumental in their decision to make Mr and Mrs McCann arguido's. However, despite there being no conclusive evidence to implicate Mr and Mrs McCann in any way with Madeleine's abduction, they had to suffer in silence the lies and smears, and a measure of public hostility, for over a year. In this time, not one scrap of further evidence was ever found. Why were they not released from this suspect status sooner?

May I ask you, if at all possible, to speak to your opposite number in Portugal, and ask that a full and proper public enquiry be conducted into the whole of the investigation into Madeleine's abduction. I ask you this as a concerned British citizen, and one who will not ever consider taking a holiday in Portugal until such time as these, and many more questions have been answered.

We gratefully acknowledge the following sources permission to use the articles, in part or in whole, below. All sources subject to copyright.

http://www.people.co.uk/news/news/tm_method=full%26objectID=20691904%26siteID=93463-name_page.html

http://www.mirror.co.uk/news/top-stories/2008/08/07/desperate-kate-mccann-s-heartbreak-letter-to-police-please-end-my-torture-115875-20687157/

http://www.mirror.co.uk/sunday-mirror/2007/09/30/exclusive-disgrace-of-madeleine-cop-98487-19870746/

We are especially grateful to the following sources who agreed to waive any copyright fees, and we give extra acknowledgement to those sources.

http://www.liverpoolecho.co.uk/liverpool-news/breaking-news/2008/08/06/madeleine-mccann-blunders-would-never-happen-in-britain-100252-21475751/

http://www.independent.co.uk/news/world/europe/police-no-breakthrough-in-search-for-madeleine-461916.html

http://abcnews.go.com/2020/Story?id=4766445&page=1

http://www.newsoftheworld.co.uk/news/article10142.ece

http://www.thesun.co.uk/sol/homepage/news/maddie/article1519421.ece

http://www.thesun.co.uk/sol/homepage/news/maddie/article1520090.ece

http://www.thesun.co.uk/sol/homepage/news/maddie/article1651651.ece

http://latestnews.virginmedia.com/news/infocus/2008/04/11/secrecy_laws_fail_to_prevent_leaks

http://www.itv.com/News/Articles/McCanns-angered-by-interview-leak-771901096.html

We acknowledge the following sources for permission to use the following pictures.

For the photo of Mr Bennett,

www.bwmaOnline.com

For the photo of Mr Amaral,

The Sun Newspaper.

For the photo of the Ocean Club,

Antonio Joao Neves.

We are especially grateful to Marcos Aragão Correia, solicitor for Leonor Cipriano, for kind permission to use the photos of Leonor, and also for giving us previously unreleased pictures of her still missing daughter, Joana.

Lightning Source UK Ltd.
Milton Keynes UK
01 December 2010

163732UK00002B/105/P

9 781438 957807